Even on Your Worst Day

YOU CAN BE
A STUDENT'S
BEST HOPE

Nately,

Stay Salty!

Even on Your Worst Day

YOU CAN BE
A STUDENT'S
BEST HOPE

— MANNY SCOTT —

ASCD | Alexandria, VA USA

1703 N. Beauregard St. • Alexandria, VA 22311-1714 USA
Phone: 800-933-2723 or 703-578-9600 • Fax: 703-575-5400
Website: www.ascd.org • E-mail: member@ascd.org
Author guidelines: www.ascd.org/write

Deborah S. Delisle, *Executive Director;* Robert D. Clouse, *Managing Director, Digital Content & Publications;* Stefani Roth, *Publisher;* Genny Ostertag, *Director, Content Acquisitions;* Julie Houtz, *Director, Book Editing & Production;* Katie Martin, *Editor;* Lindsey Smith, *Senior Graphic Designer;* Mike Kalyan, *Director, Production Services;* Circle Graphics, Inc., *Typesetter;* Kelly Marshall, *Senior Production Specialist*

PAPERBACK ISBN: 978-1-4166-2491-2   ASCD product #117077   n8/17
PDF E-BOOK ISBN: 978-1-4166-2493-6; see Books in Print for other formats.

Quantity discounts are available: e-mail programteam@ascd.org or call 800-933-2723, ext. 5773, or 703-575-5773. For desk copies, go to www.ascd.org/deskcopy.

Library of Congress Cataloging-in-Publication Data

Names: Scott, Manny, author.
Title: Even on your worst day you can be a student's best hope / Manny Scott.
Description: Alexandria, Virginia : ASCD, [2017] | Includes bibliographical
   references and index.
Identifiers: LCCN 2017026432 (print) | LCCN 2017029819 (ebook) |
   ISBN 9781416624936 (PDF) | ISBN 9781416624912 (pbk.)
Subjects: LCSH: Motivation in education. | Teacher-student relationships.
Classification: LCC LB1065 (ebook) | LCC LB1065 .S395 2017 (print) | DDC
   370.15/4—dc23
LC record available at https://lccn.loc.gov/2017026432

26 25 24 23 22 21 20 19   3 4 5 6 7 8 9 10 11 12

*I dedicate this book to Erin Gruwell,
my high school English teacher, who,
with unconditional love and unrelenting faith,
helped me turn the page and begin writing a new,
more fulfilling chapter in my life.*

Even on Your Worst Day

YOU CAN BE
A STUDENT'S
BEST HOPE

Introduction

As I travel around the country, my heart is breaking because I see so many young people who are struggling and in pain. Many of them were born into environments that have instilled in them habits that are smothering their ambition, sabotaging their success, and stunting their growth. Many of them feel hopeless, and I used to be just like them.

My father, whose father never knew him and whose mother never wanted him, has been in prison for most of my life. My mother, whose father disowned her and whose mother abandoned her, was on her own at the age of 16. Enduring things I do not have time to share here, my mother did her best to survive. It was into that world that I was born.

For much of my childhood, my mother made only $5,000 a year. We lived in 26 places before I was 16 years old—not including the cars, the beaches, the alleys, the hotels, the motels, and the homeless shelters. Sometimes I was so hungry that I jumped into dumpsters to search for food. During those times, I often became so sad that I used to cry myself to sleep at night, drenching my pillows (or the floors of our homeless shelters) with tears and hoping that my eyes would not open the next morning.

I took all of those issues with me to school. My teachers did their best to teach me, but how could I, as a little boy, care about math and integers when my personal life was full of fractures and frictions? How could I care about helping verbs at school when words never seemed to help me at home? How could I care about the different food groups the body needs to be healthy when sometimes I barely had enough food to survive? How could I focus on schoolwork when defending my mother from her crack-addicted, alcoholic boyfriend became a regular part of my home routine? And how could I care about going to school when I wasn't even sure I would have a home to go to at night?

I began spending more of my time in the streets. In fact, every year from 4th to 9th grade, I ditched school 60 to 90 days. I started stealing groceries from supermarkets just so I could have enough food to help me make it through the night. I started smoking marijuana. I started drinking alcohol. I began stealing cars and burglarizing homes. As I look back now, I realize that my personal problems were pushing me down a path that nearly destroyed me.

What made a huge difference were teachers—ordinary people with extraordinary hearts—who entered my world and lovingly guided me through some of the most difficult moments of my life. Because of their help, I was able to break the cycle of infidelity, poverty, and misery that plagued my family for generations. I am now married to a woman who is dearer to me than my own heart's blood. Together, we are raising three beautiful, smart, compassionate, globally minded children. I am the first man in my family (on my father's side) in more than a century to not cheat on his wife or abandon his children. Today, I am a pilot, an investor, an entrepreneur, a homeowner, an ordained minister, and a

PhD student. All of this was made possible by the sacrificial, selfless love of teachers and other committed adults.

There are a lot of children in the world today who are living with the pain that I used to have. I can see, like it was yesterday, the face of a boy who stopped me in the hallway after I spoke at his school. He was trembling, and his eyes showed an anguish so overwhelming that he could not speak. After I sat with him for a while, he was eventually able to share with me that earlier that day, he had walked through his front door and found his father dangling from a rope. His dad had committed suicide.

I see the face of a sobbing little girl who pulled up her shirt to show me the bruises on her body and confided in me with a shaky, desperate voice, "I'm bleeding from my private parts because the men are hurting me. They're hurting me. Please help me. Please help me!"

I see the face of a hardened young man who was reduced to tears as he tried to tell me about his baby sister, murdered at just three months old, her insides destroyed by a rapist who was also their mom's boyfriend.

Then there's the face of the young man who walked up to me, perspiring, with his head hanging and tears falling from his face. As I hugged him, blood just started gushing from his nose onto my clothes and shoes and onto the gymnasium floor. Through the blood, all he kept saying to me, over and over again, was, "Thank you, thank you, thank you, thank you. . . ."

I have thousands of stories like that weighing heavy on my heart as I write these words. Those children are living in an abyss of despair. They need hope and practical help.

With all that is already on teachers' plates—having to do more with fewer resources; having to deal with the increasing intrusion of politicians, corporations, and interest groups on their profession; and having to navigate cultural conflicts within increasingly diverse classrooms—what can teachers realistically do to help troubled children succeed in school and come out prepared for work and life?

That's what this little book is about. I share how teachers helped me overcome my environment and how they helped me go from earning Fs and Ds to As and Bs. I describe the small things they did that equipped me to take responsibility for my own success and reevaluate my relationships with people who were limiting my potential. I also share how they helped me go from being a high school dropout to a self-motivated student who has earned one graduate degree and is on the way to another. Part of my story is told in the movie *Freedom Writers* (2007), which highlights how one of those teachers—my high school English teacher, Erin Gruwell—helped me and my classmates see our own possibilities and the possibilities of the world around us.

My teachers' help for me did not stop after I left their classrooms. So I also explain how they contributed to my becoming the faithful husband and loving father I am today, even though I had never really seen up close what a good husband or father looked like. In short, I describe the seeds my teachers planted in my young mind and heart all those years ago that have produced the bounty I enjoy today.

I also share many of the things I have learned from my own experience of working with underperforming youth. Since 1999, I have been on the road up to 300 days a year, speaking primarily at conventions, conferences, and schools to nearly 2 million administrators, teachers, leaders, and students. Roughly half of those audiences were, and are, middle and high school students. In urban contexts, the students with whom I work are primarily Caucasian, African American, and Mexican American. Most of my student audiences are living at or below the poverty line. They are typically the kids that many teachers have had a hard time reaching and teaching.

Using the approaches I share in this book, I have been able to reach them, and in quite meaningful ways. For example, not too long ago, a state superintendent of public education invited me to speak in a rural school district to about 2,000 middle and high school students. During the hour I was speaking at the assembly, I sensed something special happening in the room. I learned later that after my presentation, 43 students went to counselors to confess that they had been thinking about committing suicide and admit to needing help. All of them received it.

Because of my work, I have seen many young people who were once thinking about dropping out of high school go on to college. I have seen those who were getting *F*s and *D*s turn things around academically. I have seen young people who were molested learn to view themselves as survivors and to live with zest and purpose. I have seen young people come to me with tears in their eyes and tell me that they are no longer going to cut themselves, no longer going to disrespect teachers, no longer going to dishonor their parents. I have seen real changes take place, and I am so very grateful to have played a small part in those transformations.

This book is my attempt to help people like you have this kind of impact on the young people in your school or in your classroom. I have, through a lot of trial and error, learned to do a few things well, and one of those things is connect with kids across the borders of race, class, gender, and sexual orientation. What does this entail? And how can you do it too? That's what I will try to answer in this book.

In the chapters ahead, I will do my best to share with you my understanding of how to reach young people whom others have not. My approach is a work in progress; it's not a formula, and it's not a silver bullet. It's just one way to effect positive changes in the lives of students. And although I am working on my doctorate in intercultural studies with a minor in education, this book is not written for scholars, but for people in the classroom. I am too busy right now speaking around the country and completing coursework to try to write for an academic audience. While I might one day be sitting in an ivory tower, right now, like many of you, I am working in the trenches.

As you read through this book, really slow down and reflect on how the lessons I've learned and advice I share can be applied to your own situation. If something pricks you, surprises you, upsets you, or challenges you, stop and think about it. If something causes a light bulb to go on in your head, stop reading, pull out your journal, and write. Or write in the margins here. Expand on what the words I've written mean to you, or on what they could mean for your students. That's the way for this book to be really useful. Mastering the approaches I'll lay out can take time. To be frank with you, I'm still working on several of them myself. One thing I have found, though, is that the better I get at practicing what I preach in this book, the greater my impact. I believe the same will be true for you, too.

In any case, I humbly request that you put your heart and mind into reading this book. If you honor my request, I believe you will begin to see some real breakthroughs in your teaching.

Right now,
with whatever
limitations you have,
you have the
power to change
someone's life.

1

You Can Lead Students to Water and *Make* Them Drink

I'll never forget the cowboy who changed my life.

After I finished speaking to a group of leaders and educators at a conference in Rockwall, Texas, they stood on their feet and blessed me with a long and enthusiastic ovation. After they took their seats again, I saw a raised hand in the back-left corner of the room. Someone had a question. A man rose to speak. His voice was a little shaky, indicating that he was fighting back tears.

He said, "Sir, I can't thank you enough for your presentation today. I really needed to hear that." He paused for a moment to contain his emotion before continuing, "More than you know, I really needed to hear that." Then he asked his question: "I came here looking for guidance about one kid in particular. How do you reach that kid in the back of the room who has his head down on his desk, who has difficult parents, and who is not interested in anything you have to say? How do you reach *that* kid? I want to reach that kid. Do you have any advice for me?"

Grateful for this man's transparency and his genuine concern, I thanked him, and then I gave my answer. "Sir, you can't make kids want an education," I said. "All you can do is the best you can with what you've got. It really is true that you can lead a horse to water, but you can't make—"

Before I could finish the phrase, a man in the back-right corner of the room cut me off. He had a huge cowboy hat on his head and a big, ornate, flashy buckle on his belt. He also had a really cool Texan accent, as I learned when he called out in a voice loud enough for the whole room to hear, "Excuse me, sir! I beg your pardon. I'm sorry to interrupt you, but I'm *from here.*"

I smiled and nodded, acknowledging him, his apology, and his unique flair.

"I was born on a ranch," the cowboy continued, "I was raised on a ranch, and—believe it or not—I live on a ranch right now. What you're sayin' about the horse is only partially correct. *Partially.* You see, sir, it's true that you can lead a horse to water and that won't make it drink. That's true, fair enough. What most people don't realize, though, is that you can slap some salt in that horse's mouth to make it thirsty. *Then* that horse'll drink! It's called a 'salt lick.'" The crowd erupted with laughter and applause.

This truth—that all it takes is a little salt in a horse's mouth to make it thirsty and make it drink—utterly changed how I think about teaching and leadership. Later that night, sitting alone in my hotel room, I connected this great insight to something a Jewish carpenter told his followers nearly 2,000 years ago: "You are the salt of the earth." He taught them that they, by the very essence of who they chose to be and how they chose to live their lives, had the capacity to make others thirsty . . . and, in doing so, they had the ability to change the world.

Do you realize that you too have the capacity to make your students thirsty for education? By the way you talk, by the way you walk, by the way you teach, and by the way you live, you have within you the power to make your students thirsty for learning, for knowledge, and for wisdom. Right now, with whatever limitations you have, you have the power to change someone's life. Yes, even the life of *that kid*, the one in the back of the room with his head down on his desk and the difficult home life and no apparent interest in drinking the water you're offering.

I'm convinced that the best way to bring the kind of "salt" that will make students thirsty is to prepare yourself every morning to be your absolute best. If you have not properly prepared to teach with excellence every day, then you are not honoring the commitment you made at the beginning of your teaching career to honor and educate the young minds under your care. If, for whatever reason, you have lost that zeal and the will to be your best as a teacher, then you need to find a way to reconnect with that passion and purpose. You need to reclaim your saltiness.

It is true that proper preparation prevents poor performance. The difference between success and failure as a teacher lies in the difference of habits. Teachers who have good habits do well, and those who have bad habits do poorly. There are no shortcuts to succeeding as a teacher. (I would have found them by now if there were some.) I have learned that if you want to do well as an educator (or in any area of your life), if you want to avoid teaching that is bland and boring, frustrating and flavorless, then you must start your work before your workday starts. In this chapter, I want to share with you some things to help you "get salty" and get yourself ready to teach.

Prepare Your Voice

Before you teach, you should almost always try to warm up your voice for 30 to 60 minutes. As a teacher, you are a vocal athlete. Like a great runner would do before a race, you have to warm up your (vocal) muscles before school. There are several programs and apps that you can download to help you warm up your voice. Explore them, and find one that works for you.

I have been warming up my voice before lectures, lessons, seminars, and keynotes for the past 20 years. Those vocal exercises have helped me learn to control my voice and not have it control me. If you have not warmed up your voice and you have to teach for several hours, then you risk straining it, getting hoarse and raspy, and maybe losing your voice entirely.

Prepare Your Mind

Preparing your mind for the work ahead of you is matter of learning to ask yourself the right kinds of questions. Those questions determine what you focus on, and what you focus on determines how you feel at any given moment.

Let me explain. A little while ago, I was scheduled to speak 29 times in 16 states within a 3-week period. One day, halfway through the tour, I drove more than three hours to catch a couple flights that lasted a few more hours. After the airline informed me that they had lost my luggage, I drove another hour to my hotel. I did not get to sleep until 4:30 a.m. And facing me when I awoke was a day with four scheduled speaking events in front of four large groups.

When my alarm started blaring at 5:45 a.m., do you think I felt like speaking? After getting only 75 minutes of sleep, I felt terrible. My body was still tired, and my brain was tired too. *Why?* I asked myself. *Why did I do this to myself? Why did I schedule these events so close together?* I wallowed there in my bed, feeling discouraged. The questions I was asking myself made me focus on things that made me feel even worse.

Don't miss this: *What you focus on determines how you feel at any given moment.*

So I have some important questions for you: How do you feel most of the time? Depressed? Sad? Lonely? Angry? Unappreciated? Picked on? Is it possible that some of the questions you ask yourself daily are leading you to focus on things that are making you feel terrible? Miserable? Sad?

If you want to change how you feel, you need to change your focus, and in order to change your focus, you need to change your questions. More specifically, you need to get in the habit of asking yourself the right questions in the morning. Here are some questions I ask myself each morning that I am scheduled to teach or speak, followed by my usual answers.

- **What am I grateful for today?** I am grateful to be alive today. I am grateful for health. I am grateful I heard that alarm clock. I am grateful I have an opportunity to work. I am grateful I have a sound mind.
- **Who loves me today, and whom do I love?** My wife loves me, my children love me, my mom loves me, my friends love me, my brothers love me, and God loves me. And I love them.
- **What am I proud about in my life today?** I am proud to be a great father. I am proud to be at this place in my life, doing well. I am proud that I lost 35 pounds. I am proud that I know how to fly airplanes. I am proud that I have broken so many cycles of poverty, mediocrity, and misery in my family.
- **What is the most important thing I need to get done today?** I need to connect with the people I'll be speaking to or teaching and help them realize their own potential and power to change their own lives and the lives of those around them.

What about you? What are some questions you might ask yourself to change how you feel and empower yourself to have a great day? What are some questions you can ask yourself every morning? In the afternoon? After a challenging experience? You can use my questions as a starting point, and think up some of your own.

Prepare Your Body

Some days, even after I have asked myself all of the questions above, I do not feel quite ready to teach or speak. I have learned another trick for navigating these cases: *When your mind doesn't change how you feel, your body can.*

Motion can change your emotions. In mornings before I speak or teach, I usually work out for 30 to 60 minutes. I often jog a few miles. Sometimes I lift weights or go swimming. Sometimes I get on a stair climber, and sometimes I do planks in order to strengthen my core. What I have found is that the more I get my heart pumping and my blood flowing, the better I begin feel.

I also share this to encourage you to get in shape. Stamina is basically part of a teacher's job description, and besides, you never know when you will be faced with a situation that requires you to be your best physically. Of course, there are many things in life that being in shape cannot prevent, but it's better to be able to run and not need to than to *need* to run and not be able to.

Prepare Your Heart

Finally, after making sure my voice, mind, and body are ready, I position my heart to speak, teach, and serve. Methods for this will vary. I tend to listen to music that inspires me, sing songs that encourage my heart, and pray.

I cannot even begin to describe to you how preparing my heart for work has transformed my life as a teacher and speaker. Knowing how powerful this can be, I want to encourage you to find a way to prepare your heart to teach. Maybe it's meditation or yoga or some other mindfulness approach. I have heard of some teachers looking in the mirror and speaking words of self-affirmation every morning. Some people dance in their cars on the way to work. Some teachers have told me that they find video clips that make them laugh. Others write in a journal every morning to get their hearts ready for the day. Whatever it takes, get yourself centered before you start your workday.

Nurture the Habits That Sustain You

As a teacher, there are going to be times when you will face distractions, deterrents, and all sorts of obstacles. In those times, it will be your habits that will keep you at your best. Without good habits, you will surrender; with good habits, you will survive.

Let me tell you about a time that my habits helped to sustain me. I was scheduled to speak eight times in two days to eight large groups of students and school employees. While I knew the work would be hard, I had no idea exactly *how* challenging those two days would be. After each of the four middle or high school assemblies, I talked to thousands of students, one on one, listening attentively to their stories, encouraging them to do their best in school, and patiently helping them persevere through their pain. To be fully present with each person requires a stamina and strength that is hard to describe.

Furthermore, during a couple of my presentations to auditoriums and gymnasiums of adults, the microphones died on me. The technology team was unable to fix the problem, so I had to project my voice loudly for nearly two hours so that everyone could hear me.

It was because I put myself in my "salty" zone by waking up early each day to prepare my voice, mind, body, and heart that I was able to make it through those two days without losing my effectiveness. To be sure, every fiber of my being was aching from exhaustion after all eight presentations. Still, I could walk away from those engagements with the certainty that I had done my absolute best to create an unquenchable thirst in my audiences.

When you are fully committed to helping others as a teacher, you are going to do the things that most other people will not do. You are going to have to make sacrifices that others are not willing to make. You are going to have to train your voice, mind, body, and heart to perform at maximal levels.

I have been teaching for nearly 20 years, and I have no doubt that my private habits have led to my public effectiveness. They have allowed me to not only survive but thrive. They help me sustain the salt I need to be effective. I share that not to impress you, but to impress upon you that I would not be the teacher or speaker I am without the habits I have developed: the tens of thousands of hours that I have spent studying, writing, and preparing for my presentations; exercising before dawn; warming up my voice; and centering myself so that I can teach with clarity, conviction, passion, and power.

My friend, commit to a daily morning routine that will make you salty. Diligently prepare your voice, mind, body, and heart to be your absolute best so that you can inspire in your students a thirst for knowledge and wisdom that they will never outgrow and never forget.

Knowing content
and pedagogy
is not enough.

2

It Starts with Relationships

The other kids in my 6th grade class were laughing and having a good time, but I couldn't even find it in myself to smile. I sat there numb. Calloused. Hardened.

The night before, I had heard the sound of crashing glass and my mother letting out a terrifying, heart-wrenching scream. In a panic, I ran to our apartment door and opened it to see my stepfather in the hallway, holding my mother by the back of her head, by her hair. I saw blood pouring down my mother's neck, soaking through her blouse. My stepfather had just slammed my mother's head through the large glass window that was in the hallway of our building. So I did my best to intervene, to fight a grown man. I lost, of course. It was a long night of paramedics, police officers, and pain.

The very next day, with almost no sleep, I went to school. Although I was present physically, I was absent mentally. On the playground, I looked around at the other kids and wondered to myself, *Why does everyone seem so happy? What's so funny? What is there to laugh and be happy about?*

My teachers didn't make things any better for me that day. I remember sitting in class, wearing clothes that probably hadn't been washed in a month or two. The shoes on my feet were too big and full of holes, hand-me downs from my older brothers.

My teacher asked a question, and even though several of my classmates raised their hands to answer and I did not, she called on me. She asked, "Why don't you give it a try? What do you think the answer is?"

I shrank in my chair.

"You did your homework last night, didn't you?" she said.

I answered honestly. "No, ma'am. I tried, but I didn't understand it."

Then, in a very condescending tone, she asked, "Nobody at home could help you with your homework? *Nobody?*"

I felt terrible. "No, ma'am. They didn't understand it either."

She rolled her eyes. "Stand up," she said. Already feeling stupid for not understanding the homework, I stood up. Then she asked, "Why do your clothes look like that?"

Her question knocked the wind out of me. I just looked down at my shirt and my raggedy pants and my too-big shoes with the holes in them. Then I looked back up at her.

"Don't you have a washing machine at home?" she continued.

"No, ma'am," I said, shaking my head.

"Come with me," she ordered. She took me out to the hallway, just outside the door, and said, "Your clothes stink. The other kids are complaining that you are stinking up the classroom."

The shame was so torturous that I couldn't even mumble a response.

"Why do your clothes look like this?" she repeated. "You don't have a washing machine at home?"

"No, ma'am," I said again, because what else could I say?

My teacher then proceeded to predict my future. "If you don't get your act together and start doing your homework, you are not going to graduate from school," she told me. "You are probably going to go to prison, and you are probably going to end up just like your father." Then, with a little grin, she asked, "Isn't he in prison or something?"

Looking back on this now, the most charitable interpretation I can give is that my teacher simply did not know the harm she was inflicting. Her white, Midwestern, middle-class frame of reference was not inherently bad, but it held that every family had a washing machine, ate three healthy meals a day, and was headed by parents who had the time and education to help their kids with homework. It blinded her to my pain, to the absurdity that everything could be different for me if I just decided to get my act together, and to the humiliation she was inflicting. This teacher failed to understand that she didn't just teach reading, writing, or math; she taught reading *to kids*, she taught writing *to kids*, she taught math *to kids*. And not just to kids, but to kids like me, who led very different lives from her own.

That experience taught me that poverty is more than the lack of money; poverty is also the lack of access to people who can help you flourish in life. As a kid living in poverty, it was so discouraging to realize that so few people wanted more for me, believed in me, and wanted to help me become somebody. I couldn't even count on the teachers in my school. It was then, in 6th grade, that I decided I was no longer going to subject myself to that kind of rejection, misery, and shame. It was because of that hallway conversation that I decided to start ditching school.

I share this story with you because there are probably many young people who attend your school who have experienced the kind of pain and abuse and ostracism and embarrassment that I experienced as a little boy. They might be seeing their mothers get beaten. They might be homeless. They might have been humiliated by some of their other teachers and classmates. As a result, they are on the verge of giving up on school, of dropping out. And you might be the one person who can change their minds. You might be the person they need to help them turn the page and begin a new, healthier, and more fulfilling chapter in their lives.

But how? If 6th grade me were sitting in your classroom—exhausted, traumatized, unprepared to learn, wearing the same unwashed clothes day after day—what would you do?

I am absolutely convinced that the most important thing you can do as a teacher is strive to build a relationship with each of your students. For children growing up in violent or impoverished environments, this is especially critical. It can be a lifeline. I know, because it was a lifeline for me.

My 11th grade English teacher, Erin Gruwell, grew up in a white, upper-middle-class family, and she taught students who were generally black, Latino, and Asian. Most of us lived in neighborhoods with a lot of gang violence and poverty. Culturally and socioeconomically, our teacher was worlds apart from us, and yet she was still able to reach most of us. Why? Because she did the work necessary to build healthy relationships with us. Ms. G realized what all teachers who hope to work well cross-culturally must: *Knowing content and pedagogy is not enough.* She learned how to enter into her students' lives with openness and acceptance so that she could build trust. You must do this, too.

Openness

Many of your students have been hurt. As a result, they have crossed their arms and closed themselves off from being open, vulnerable, or receptive to new people and experiences. They do not feel safe. They do not feel welcome.

The way to address that is by embodying openness.

The people who changed my life are those who embodied openness in the best way. My former professor Dr. Duane Elmer once said in class, "Openness is the ability to welcome people into your presence so that they feel safe and secure." When you embody openness, you have a posture about you, a demeanor that makes others feel at ease. When you embody openness, your eyes smile when you see your students. When they come into your presence, you greet them with sincere kindness, and your warmth lifts their spirits. Students feel safe and secure when they can see, in your eyes and body language, and hear in your voice that you are genuinely happy to see them.

I met a teacher in Columbia, South Carolina, who said that she had been having problems with the school lunch lady but did not know why. After talking to the lunch lady and then to a few trusted friends, she concluded that she was coming off as a rude and mean person, even though that was never her intention. She explained to me that she was an introvert and she hadn't realized that others perceived her introversion as distant and unfriendly. After this epiphany, she worked to become more open to others, both colleagues and students.

Do you come off as open to others? Or do you come off as someone who is closed off? Is it possible people perceive you to be rude, abrasive, or cold? It would not hurt (well, it might hurt a little) to ask some people whose opinion you value and hear their perceptions of how you relate to others. Their revelations might help you to grow.

Another teacher I met recently told me that she had been feeling down, drained, and depressed. She felt sapped of joy and unmotivated in the classroom. Then, she explained, one day she just decided that she was going change her attitude about her job. She vowed to try greeting each day with love in her heart and gratitude for the little things. That little shift altered everything for her. She now walks onto her campus more open, enthusiastic, and ready to learn and teach.

I will be the first to admit that embodying openness and being fully present with students is not always easy. For the last two years, my wife and I have homeschooled our children because I travel so much for work and we want to keep our family together. However, sometimes, while teaching them math, language arts, social studies, or science, I get preoccupied by some of my other obligations. I know this is happening when I find myself getting frustrated by my children's questions or their need for help with an assignment. Because busyness prevents me from embodying openness, I have to constantly work at it. It's hard with three students, so I know it is exponentially more challenging with a classroom full of kids!

When you are teaching, I want to encourage you to do whatever you need to do to become more emotionally and mentally available to your students.

Acceptance

Another thing teachers can do is work to develop acceptance, or tolerance, for others. Now let me be clear: Acceptance does not mean agreeing with or celebrating everyone's every choice, behavior, or idea. When I talk about acceptance, I am referring to the ability to continue seeing the beauty and value of your students despite their "issues." Acceptance means being able to continue holding your students in high regard even though you see their shortcomings. It's the ability to continue seeing their potential even though you see their problems.

The life I have led has taught me the sad truth that most people *love* you until they *know* you. It's taught me that love can often be very conditional. People will love you when you are dressed up, when you are paying for their meals, when you agree with them, when you meet their standards. However, when people see the imperfect parts of you—your character flaws, your brokenness, your bad attitude, or your insecurity—they tend to distance themselves.

However, the people who changed my life, many of them teachers, saw my issues and insecurities and inadequacies and—after they had really gotten to *know* me—still loved me. They kept faith in me and did not stop supporting me, investing in me. They saw that I did not know how to study, but they also saw a potential college graduate. They noticed that I had a bad temper, but they also saw someone who could one day learn to channel that anger in a positive way. They saw someone who had several character flaws, but they also saw someone who could achieve great things. They recognized my problems, but they did not hold them against me. Instead, they saw both who I was and who I might become and kept calling me up to this potential. That is acceptance.

Can you love someone whose behavior you do not like? Can you accept someone who has bad habits? When that young person comes into your classroom with a bad attitude and doesn't want to talk to you, can you still see worth and value, even if you are frustrated? Can you accept the young person who has his head down on his desk, the one who didn't do her homework, the one who recently got suspended for getting into an altercation?

A kindergarten teacher told me a story about one of her kids who had a lot of issues. When she greeted this little boy as he walked into class one day, he lashed out at her, saying, "You're ugly, you're stupid, and you're fat." Here's how she responded: "Sounds like somebody needs a hug! Come here!" And she commenced to squeeze him. *That's* what acceptance looks like. It is giving others permission to be imperfect. To be sure, I am not saying that you should allow people to mistreat you or say mean and hurtful things to you. I *am* saying, however, that when people say or do hurtful things to you, it's on you to be mature enough to realize that their hostility probably has very little to do with you. It's far more likely that this student (or adult) is going through some very difficult things. Acceptance is giving people permission to have bad moments.

Practicing acceptance will open so many doors for you as a teacher. Loving others when they feel unlovable will break down so many barriers. Your students will be surprised and shocked. They'll wonder, *Why is this person treating me this way? Why are they still nice to me, even though I haven't been nice to them?*

Here is what you're doing when you practice acceptance. You're saying, "Yes, I see your brokenness. Yes, I see your shortcomings. Yes, I see your character flaws. Yes, I know your mother said you were a liability and that you were not going to succeed in life. But I say different. I see something great in you. Yes, I know your father has been gone, leaving you without a role model for how to be a man. Yes, I know that you have been irresponsible. But I still love you and believe in you. Yes, I understand that some things happened to you in your life that hurt you, but I still see a high school graduate. I see a doctor. I see a lawyer. I see a teacher. I see an engineer. I see someone who can be happily married. I see someone who can one day be a great father or a great mother. *I see someone who can make a big difference in this world.*"

When you speak, in word or deed, these assurances into the lives of students who are living beneath their potential, you will be well on your way to cultivating a healthy relationship with them.

Trust

Finally, as a teacher, if you embody openness and acceptance, you will be in a position to establish trust.

Odds are that in your classroom, there is at least one student who has felt betrayed or abandoned so many times that his or her heart cannot bear the idea of being hurt by anyone else. To protect themselves, children in these situations put up emotional walls to keep people from getting close to them. In order to get your students to let down their guards and tear down their emotional walls, you must learn how to develop trust. Trust is mutual confidence; it's what allows people to believe that they are acting in one another's best interest. When someone you trust hurts or disappoints you, you have the confidence that they did not do it on purpose, and, if you hurt or disappoint them, they are sure that you did not do it on purpose either.

I met a teacher who once baked a birthday cake for one of her students. Surprised, he thanked her, and walked away with his cake. The next day, she saw this boy at his locker, and in his locker was the birthday cake. Uneaten. Untouched, in fact. She gently asked why, and he replied that no one had ever given him a birthday cake, and so he didn't want to ruin it. Her little act of generosity was, for him, a momentous event. He went on to become one of her best students.

I met another teacher who was about 70 years old and was having an amazing impact on his kids. When I asked him to reveal his secrets to me, he said that he picked one or two students a day to privately encourage. He wrote them little notes, gave them little gifts, or spent a little extra time speaking positive words to them. He told me, "Manny, I don't know how much longer I have to live. My wife died recently. With the time I have left, I just want my students to know that I care about them, that they matter to me, that I love them." The students at that school loved that man. They trusted him. It was a beautiful thing to see. His little acts of kindness had a tremendous effect on his kids and on me. His kids were white, Latino, black, and Asian. They were rich and poor. And they all trusted him.

Trust doesn't come about by accident; you have to be intentional about building it. In this age of skepticism and doubt, so many young people have their guards up. They are afraid of being betrayed, backstabbed, and let down. We've seen some examples of one way to build trust—just doing little things for students that let them know that you care about them. Add to those practices positive actions like sending a handwritten note to their parents or guardians about how well they have done in class or on an assignment, or writing some sincere and thoughtful words of encouragement on an assignment or journal entry. Give students birthday cards, signed by you and maybe even by the rest of the class. Attend their extracurricular events, or give them a compliment in front of their parents, other adults, or other students.

Talk of public compliments and acknowledgments reminds me to pause to note that there are cultural considerations to keep in mind. In collectivistic contexts, as opposed to predominantly individualistic contexts, celebrating an individual's success or effectiveness may lead the group to punish the individual—and undercut your efforts at building trust. One of the benefits of individualism is that it encourages the individual to achieve his or her potential; one of its challenges, however, is that it does not concern itself with the well-being of the group. Collectivism is just the opposite: The individual exists for the well-being of the group regardless of the individual's personal preferences. In contexts where the group takes priority over the individual, usually the group flourishes as a whole. The challenge of growing up in such a context, however, is that the individual often does not achieve his or her own personal potential. Ideally, you want to teach people in an individualistic context that they should also be concerned about the well-being of others, and teach people in collectivistic contexts to encourage individuals to be their absolute best (because it helps all of us). So, in collectivistic contexts, rather than publicly celebrate an individual for being successful, it can be wiser to talk publicly about how that success honors the entire group. Then, when the opportunity presents itself, you can encourage some of your outstanding students privately. It's an approach where everyone wins. Regardless of the kind of environment you're teaching in, whether individual-centered or group-centered, think carefully about how you choose to highlight the success of your students. The last thing you want to do is cause them to lose face or social standing.

No matter what small actions you decide to take to build trust, do not underestimate their power. Little things can have a big impact on building trusting relationships.

Take Action to Build Relationships

Openness, acceptance, and trust are the three pillars of solid relationships with students (and with everyone, really). Doing the work of helping students feel safe and secure in your presence; demonstrating that you love them as whole people, even with their shortcomings; and cultivating their confidence in you as someone who has their best interests at heart will open the door to more effective teaching. By embodying openness, acceptance, and trust, you position yourself to begin learning about, from, and with your students in ways that will transform your life and theirs.

Invest as
much time in
understanding *who*
you teach as you do
in understanding
what you teach.

3

Become a Student of Your Students

I want to talk now about the school that compelled me to change the way I teach and speak. It was on the South Side of Chicago, in a predominantly black neighborhood called Bronzeville that was being punished by poverty and crippled by crime. Known in the early 20th century as "Black Metropolis," this area was once home to many black-owned businesses and prominent African Americans. A lot has changed there since the 1960s, when the Chicago Housing Authority built poorly constructed public housing projects that exacerbated poverty and stoked severe social problems.

The principal of the school was on a mission to improve student performance. She contacted me, explaining that she believed I could help inspire her students to not only survive their difficult circumstances but also thrive in school, work, and life.

As I walked through the front doors, I was met by an armed police officer. He asked me to sign my name on his clipboard, empty my pockets, and pass through the metal detector. Once I had gathered my belongings, I was greeted by the school's principal. While she escorted me to the auditorium, she tried to explain, almost desperately, how much her students needed to be inspired, encouraged, and empowered. She said that many of them were apathetic about academics and had very little respect for themselves, their classmates, or their teachers.

The buzz of a room full of loud and somewhat rowdy students hit me before we reached the auditorium. I heard someone on the microphone trying quiet them down, but they were ignoring her. My heart rate began to speed up, because I knew that they were going to be a challenging group. As it turned out, "challenging" was an understatement.

My audience that day was about 1,000 black students. Most of them were talking to the people sitting around them. Some of them had headphones on. Some were yelling across the room to their friends. Most of them just seemed glad to be out of class, even if it was to sit in an assembly to listen to a guest speaker.

I watched the principal take the stage. "Students, may I have your attention, please?" she called out. After about 30 seconds of repeating herself, most of the room quieted down enough to hear what she had to say. "We have a special guest today," she continued. "So please turn off your phones, don't talk to your neighbors, and please, please, *please* give him your undivided attention." (Her repeated pleas only made me more concerned about how they would treat me.) With a raised, hopeful voice, she said, "Please clap your hands and help me welcome Mr. Manny Scott!"

About 10 people clapped. The rest just stared at me as I walked onstage. They wanted to know if I was going to be worth their time.

I greeted them with a warm "Good morning," but they remained quiet. I told them that I was happy to be there and grateful for the opportunity to speak to them. Then I proceeded to deliver a speech I was accustomed to giving to adults. I told them about the neighborhoods I grew up in, a little bit about my family, and about the background of the movie *Freedom Writers*, which featured a character partly based on me, and whose story very much resembled mine.

The students were quiet during the first few minutes of my presentation, but the longer I talked, the harder it was for me to keep their attention. When I told a joke that always worked with my accustomed audience, a few of the students in the audience laughed—but they laughed at *me*, not at the joke. I could tell that I was losing them, but I did not understand why. So I tried harder and spoke with more intensity, but that didn't work either. Even though I was giving them my absolute best, they could not have cared less about what I was saying. At the end of presentation, probably the same 10 people who had clapped for me at the beginning clapped again. I think they were all teachers.

Afterward, the principal took me to the cafeteria to meet with the students on a more personal level. When I walked in, they pretty much ignored me. Not one student came up to me to shake my hand or to thank me for my presentation. Not one of them seemed to have been moved by anything I had said. It was one of the most humbling experiences I have ever had in my professional life.

After lunch, I walked to my car with my tail between my legs. I was confused. I had pretty much flunked that presentation and made absolutely no difference in the lives of those students. The reflection continued on my drive home, with me wracking my brain, trying to understand what had happened. First, I blamed the students. *They were just bad kids who had no home training,* I said to myself. *Maybe they weren't smart enough to understand what I was trying to tell them. Oh well, they'll learn the hard way.* However, something inside me, perhaps my conscience, was telling me that blaming them was not the answer. I searched my soul for a better explanation. If I was going to continue speaking to students in neighborhoods like that, then I needed to identify the core cause of my failure so I could correct it. What I was really wondering was this: *Why didn't those kids care about what I had to say?*

Eventually, this truth hit me hard: My presentation had flopped because I had not figured out how to connect to my audience. I had assumed that despite some minor differences, like age and where we grew up, those kids and I were basically alike. We thought the same, felt the same, and behaved in essentially the same way. I could not have been more wrong in my assessment.

This experience taught me that a lack of awareness of one's own cultural particularity or ethnocentricity can lead us to wrongly attribute students' resistance to their moral failures rather than to our own cultural incompetence. When I was speaking to those students in Chicago, and they were shutting out my message, the problem wasn't them—it was me. More pointedly, it was how I had not taken the time to understand them.

It is indispensable for all teachers to become a student of their students, and learning about their culture is a huge part of that challenge. In fact, you should probably invest as much time in understanding *who* you teach as you do in understanding *what* you teach. In the absence of such work, you risk creating chasms between you and your students that will make it nearly impossible for you teach them effectively. Even worse, if you try to teach students you don't understand, you can become a benevolent oppressor.

For an example of what I mean by that, let me tell you about a presentation I recently attended where a white teacher was speaking about the Emancipation Proclamation, the document President Abraham Lincoln signed to abolish slavery (mainly to preserve the union). In his remarks, this teacher painted a very romantic picture of "the Old South" and how some enslaved people preferred slavery to freedom. He told an emotional story, with tears in his eyes, of a black woman who, despite being freed by Lincoln, returned to her plantation and ran back into the arms of her white slavemaster because he treated her so well. She said that slavery wasn't as bad as some people believed and that she would never leave her master's side again.

While several white people in the audience seemed unbothered by the illustration, I looked around at the other black audience members to see if I was the only one who was in disbelief about what I had just heard. I was not. The face of almost every black person with whom I made eye contact displayed anger, disappointment, confusion, or pain. What that teacher failed to realize is that many black people have older members in our families who still have the stench of slavery and discrimination on them, and who have told us their heartbreaking stories of how they saw, with their very own eyes, family and friends get lynched, raped, and murdered by racist white mobs. I have no doubt in my mind that that white teacher meant well when he was teaching about the Emancipation Proclamation. Still, with that kind of cultural incompetence, or lack of awareness and knowledge about his black audience members, he did real harm. He lost all credibility with us. By perpetuating a false, romanticized narrative about how many black people preferred being slaves, that white teacher was acting as a benevolent oppressor. I should add that black teachers can also become benevolent oppressors if they are teaching the same kinds of lessons to their students.

In the same way, you as a teacher can mean well but still do harm. If you are investing in the lives of your students, whom you see on a regular basis, but have not taken the time to understand who they are and how they think, feel, and behave, then you could actually do more harm than good.

Teacher, Message, Students

At its core, teaching involves communicating a message to a student. More specifically, the teacher is the educator who encodes her or his thoughts and transmits them through a message to a student, the recipient of the message. Let's go a little deeper.

The Teacher

That's you, of course. You were raised in a particular place (in a house or apartment, on a street, in a neighborhood, in a city, a state, a region, a country, and a continent) at a particular time in history (end of the 20th and the beginning of the 21st century). You learned to speak a particular language and dialect from people (your family, friends, and teachers) who shared your patterns of thinking, feeling, and behaving. Those patterns are what anthropologists refer to as *culture*. Culture, as I understand it, refers to a group's learned, shared, and integrated patterns of thinking, feeling, and behaving.

Because all of us have patterns of thinking, feeling, and behaving that we learned from and share with others from our own backgrounds, we are all culturally conditioned and linguistically particular. I've heard people express with great sincerity the idea that their patterns of belief and behavior are the default; that they are "normal" or "regular," and it's others who are "cultural" or "ethnic" or "different." This perspective is only really possible in the most homogenous of settings, where everyone around you really does share your cultural background. For teachers, who are so often surrounded by a great diversity of students, it's a destructive perspective that will only make your task more difficult.

So, as a teacher, you have objectives that you are charged with helping your students achieve. You want them to think, feel, know, or do something as a result of your time together. However, because they cannot read your mind, you must encode a message—design your instruction—and then transmit it to them in a way that will connect with and be effective for them, who are different from you. This is where teaching can become really challenging.

The Message

In order to teach a lesson, a teacher must select ideas and encode them into a message for students using words, speech, drawings, sounds, facial expressions, body language, and so on. For a teacher surrounded by students who have a common culture that she shares, the process of encoding is fairly automatic. She can give more attention to formulating her message (what she is going to say) than to encoding it (how she will say it). When a teacher is a cultural outlier, however, both the "what" and "how" of message transmission need careful attention, or many students simply will not understand.

For example, when I was a little boy, I lived in Denver, Colorado. In Denver, we referred to Coca-Cola or Pepsi as "pop" (as in, "I want a pop"). However, when I moved to Long Beach, California, people didn't know what I was talking about when I asked for a pop. After I explained that I wanted a Coke, Sprite, or Seven-Up, they usually replied, "Oh! You want a *soda*." Similarly, folks in Colorado who had dry skin that needed moisturizing asked for "cream"; in Long Beach, what they wanted was "lotion."

People in Denver and Long Beach not only used *different* words to refer to the *same* things, but they also used the *same* words to refer to *different* things. In Denver, my friends sometimes called me "bud" (short for "buddy"), but in Long Beach, they called me "homie" (or "homeboy") or "boss." In Atlanta, using "cowboy" language, some of my friends have called me "hoss." In Denver, when people said it was "cold," they were usually talking about the sub-zero temperatures or someone's distant attitude. However, in Long Beach, when people used the word "cold," they were often referring to someone's superior skill. "That guy's karate is cold," meant "that guy is really good at karate." The words people use, the ways they use them, and the different accents with which they use them are very linguistically particular.

Furthermore, whenever we speak, *most* of what we communicate is not through our words but through our nonverbal behaviors. While scholars cannot agree on exactly how much of our communication is nonverbal, most conclude that more than 70 percent of what we say is nonverbal. So the *paraverbal*—the audible sounds that we use in our oral interactions to convey meaning—speaks volumes. By the use of audible cues like volume, accent, emphasis, rhythm, inflection, intonation, and other sounds, the very same sentence can express excitement, commands, information, sadness, questions, and so much more. In English, for example, we usually inflect our voices upward at the end of questions, whereas in Spanish, it would not be uncommon for declarative sentences to end with such vocal inflection. The sounds we make are powerful in communication.

We also communicate through action and inaction. What kinds of sources or stories or examples do you use or not use during your lesson plans? What kinds of images are or are not included on the posters that decorate your classroom walls? What kinds of stories do you include or not include? I ask about these "nots" because you can communicate your feeling about something by overlooking or omitting it. If

African American or Latino American or Asian American or female examples, figures, illustrations, posters, and so on do not feature in your instruction, you are communicating that you do not think they are relevant or important. You are teaching that you do not think that African Americans or Latino Americans or Asian Americans or women have contributed anything of significance to our world. *You can communicate a whole lot by what you do not say or do.*

The environment you create is communicating something all the time. For example, when I was in college, I used to meet weekly with one of my professors and a group of my classmates in order to discuss some of our readings. I had met with them weekly for about three months, when one day during our meeting, a topic came up that made me uncomfortable. Being the only African American in the group who had grown up in the inner city, I had a perspective that was very different from theirs, because they had grown up in either the suburbs or rural areas. When I expressed my perspective on the topic, the nonverbal response of my classmates was not very affirming. People were looking at me like I was dumb. I had seen that face many times before. To make matters even worse, because I had had a long history of feeling misunderstood and unwelcome in classroom environments, I felt devastated. Neither the professor nor any of my classmates expressed any appreciation for my perspective. Instead, they all stopped talking to me for the rest of the class. I felt like they were saying that I and my perspective were not welcome. Consequently, that was the last time I attended the weekly meetings. By not showing up to their weekly meetings, I was communicating to them that I did not feel like I belonged in the group.

When some of your students (or their parents) do not show up to your class or to school, they might be saying something that you or your school need to hear. They might be saying that they do not feel valued, safe, respected, or loved. They might be saying, "You do not care about me."

The fact is, whenever we speak, we providing a window into our personal experiences, our cultural background, and our vocabularies. The way we translate our thoughts into messages can reveal everything from geographic origin to gender, age, position in society, past experiences, present emotional states, and our purpose for communicating. Yes, whenever you stand before a group of students, and try to teach them, be mindful that you are communicating some things that are beyond your intent and even beyond your control. This is why it's so important to be mindful of the other aspects of your message—how what you are saying or doing can either aid or obstruct your ability to connect with your students and teach the lessons that you would like to teach them.

The Students

The students in your classroom are responsible for decoding the message you deliver. While you might intend for them to receive a very particular meaning, ultimately, it's they who have the power. Each of them will determine for himself or herself the meaning of the message you transmit. In the end, teaching is not about what we say but about how students interpret what we say. Even a teacher speaking from a place of innate understanding and with the most supernal eloquence will be ineffective without an understanding of the language and culture of the students listening. The message will be unheard, just as mine was when I was talking to those students on the South Side of Chicago.

Awareness, Understanding, and Skill

Because teaching ultimately depends on how our students interpret what we say and do, it is imperative to develop cultural self-awareness, an understanding of our students, and the necessary skill in applying that understanding as we teach.

The key to the first challenge is to acknowledge that, as teachers, we are culturally different from our students. Even if we have the same skin color as they do, and even if we grew up in circumstances that were similar to theirs, the fact that we have gone to college, become educated, and decided on a teaching career sets our experiences apart from theirs. In all likelihood, you were born and raised and educated in a different time from them and in a different place. You grew up speaking a different dialect and have particular patterns of thinking, feeling, and behaving, informed by your unique life experiences, which are different from theirs. As such, you would be wise to get clarity about just how culturally distant you are from your students before you begin crafting your messages for them.

The Cultural Distance Calculator shown here can be a useful tool in this effort. Assign yourself a rating in each of its categories, with "1" indicating the most difference and "10" the least. Giving yourself a "10" means that you and your students are almost exactly alike in that particular area.

Add up all your ratings, and divide the total by 9. If you total score is between 8 and 10, you are very culturally near to

Cultural Distance Calculator

How similar are your and your students' . . .	1	2	3	4	5	6	7	8	9	10
Neighborhoods?										
Social structures?										
Day-to-day social interactions?										
Language/dialects?										
Ways of thinking, analyzing, evaluating, and problem solving?										
Motivators?										
Goals?										
Media influences?										
Overall worldview, regarding God, reality, knowledge, values, and the nature of human beings?										

For more about these categories, see pages 52–61.

your students. If it's between 5 and 7, you are similar to your students in a lot of ways, but you also have some important cultural differences. If you score between 1 and 4, then you and your students have significant cultural differences. Yes, the work of building bridges into the lives of your students is more challenging the further away your respective starting locations are, and that's because you've got to get yourself on a more equal cultural footing before you can begin. It can be daunting, but it's doable; you just need to equip yourself properly.

To be sure, even our best understandings of our students will be proximal, meaning they will never be perfect. That should not discourage us, however, because every day we are with students is an opportunity to acquire a better and deeper understanding of them. In the next chapter, I will explain how to use what you know about your students to be a better teacher; for the rest of this chapter, however, I want to focus on how to become a better student of your students. It's the foundation for what comes next.

Your Students' World

I believe that the best teaching comes through not only studying the world of our students but living in it. It's the surest way to see it the way they do.

While I understand there are circumstances that can make it necessary for teachers to live far away from the neighborhoods in which they teach, when you live in the same neighborhood as your students, you are positioned to familiarize yourself with their culture much more naturally. You'll learn about important or dramatic occurrences in their lives as they happen.

If, for whatever reason, you cannot live where you teach, then you must be very intentional in finding other ways to learn about your students' world. For example, you could ask your students to give you a tour of their neighborhoods. You could use journal prompts to elicit information about it. You might even want to conduct informal interviews with your students, individually, in small groups, or with the entire class. Whatever you do, find a way to get as close to their world, and their culture, as possible.

Clifford Geertz (1977) was an American anthropologist who defined "culture" in a way that was truly enlightening for me, and might be for you as well:

> Believing, with Max Weber, that man is an animal suspended in webs of significance he himself has spun, I take culture to be those webs, and the analysis of it to be therefore . . . an interpretive [science] in search of meaning. (p. 5)

Geertz is saying that when we look at how other people think, feel, and behave, what we're seeing is a representation of something that's much more deeply rooted. The way to get at the culture these patterns represent is for us to carefully study the patterns themselves.

This has powerful implications for teachers and leaders. I recently met a high school principal who was hired by a school in a very poor neighborhood. He had moved from another state to take the job. In order to learn as much as he possibly could about the culture of his students and their families, he decided to shop where they shopped, to get haircuts at their local barbershops, and to hang out in areas where they hung out. It worked. He began to understand his new community's patterns, neighborhoods, and dialect.

When opportunities presented themselves, the principal was intentional about introducing himself to the people and parents of the community, letting them know who he was and assuring them that he was there for them, their children, and their community as a resource and an advocate. He told me the community has accepted him with open arms.

They see him not as an outsider but as someone they can trust. After the first year, he said, his school has made dramatic improvements academically and socially. That principal attended to the culture of people connected with this school, and it made a big difference for him and for them.

A Seven-Point Cultural Curriculum

Choosing to see our students' patterns of thinking, feeling, and behaving as signifiers gives us a way to begin bridging cultural differences. Their words, gestures, clothing choices, favorite music, ways of being with family and friends, and so on present themselves as words on a page; if we read them carefully, we can gain a better understanding.

I recommend teachers study seven things about their students, many of which I touched on earlier in this chapter: (1) the social structures that shape students' lives, (2) their day-to-day personal interactions, (3) their language/dialect, (4) their cognitive processes, (5) their motivational influences, (6) their goals, and (7) their media influences.

1. Study Students' Social Structures

Social structures can tell us about the basic organization of students' lives and give a big-picture look at the world they live in and the influences it is imparting. Here are some of the important questions to answer:

- Where do they live? What is their neighborhood like, in general? What are its physical boundaries?
- How is their neighborhood organized? Who lives where? What are the social boundaries?

- Where do they sit at lunch? With whom do they sit?
- Who are their leaders within the school? Who are their heroes outside of it?
- At school, how do they form peer groups? How do they join groups that already exist?
- Within their peer groups, how is power distributed? Who is in charge? Who are the subordinates? Can you figure out how and why power has been distributed the way it is?
- What is their cultural background (African, African American, Salvadoran, Korean, etc.), and how influential is that background on their day-to-day life? Who are the authority figures within the culture? What are the traditional roles of men and women, older people and younger people, parents and children? How do people dress in the culture, and is there any particular article of clothing that is unique or especially significant to them?
- How does one become a member of the culture? (For example, how does a white man or woman become an accepted member of a predominantly black community, or vice versa?)
- Within the culture, is social status something achieved or is it ascribed by others? What does one have to do to enjoy high social status?
- What are the rules of the culture? What is right? What is wrong?
- How do those who break the rules get treated or punished? What are the formal and informal sanctions of their groups?
- What are the common activities, events, rituals, or customs of the culture?
- How do members of the culture use time? How do they organize their days and nights?

- What are the objects and artifacts of the culture? How do those objects get used? What is the significance of those objects and artifacts?
- How are students' families structured? Two parents, single parent? Are their families patriarchal or matriarchal?
- Within peer groups and families, how are male members expected to think, feel, and behave?
- Within peer groups and families, how are female members expected to think, feel, and behave?
- Do individuals within the culture prioritize their own goals (an individualistic culture) or the goals of their peer group or family (a collectivist culture)?
- How does emotion get expressed in the culture? Is being demonstrative encouraged or discouraged?

2. Study Students' Day-to-Day Social Interactions

In addition to studying the overarching social structures that shape your students, pay attention to the day-to-day personal interactions among members of the groups they belong to. Here are some answers to seek:

- How do they greet one another? What words, facial expressions, gestures, and body language do they use?
- How close do they stand to one another when they are in a conversation?
- How do superiors interact with their subordinates, and vice versa?
- When they are happy, how do they express that happiness? Through facial expressions? Words or sounds? Dancing?
- When they are sad, how can you tell? How do they express sadness?
- How do they express anger?

- How do arguments usually start? What is their body language during arguments? What do they do with their hands, feet, clothes, jewelry, hair?
- When there is a conflict within a group, how do members of the group address it?

3. Study Students' Language

Understanding how your students use language can provide insight into their mental and linguistic worlds. Here are some questions you should try to answer:

- What language(s) do they speak?
- What dialect(s) do they speak? How would you describe it?
- What words or phrases do they use to greet one another?
- What are some sounds that they make when talking?
- What are some phrases that they commonly use?
- Do they communicate directly or indirectly?
- What are some stories that they all know?
- How would they tell the story of their history?

4. Study How Students Think

Look for patterns in how students think about things. Richard Nisbett (2003), a professor at the University of Michigan, studies how culture influences what we value. He argues, for example, that Eastern (Asian) and Western cultures think differently from one another, with Eastern cultures prioritizing the group and Western cultures prioritizing the individual. Eastern cultures emphasize holism, interdependence, and harmony, while Western cultures think in a more linear manner and see objects in isolation, without much consideration for the context in which those objects are situated.

Furthermore, Sharan B. Merriam, in *Non-Western Perspectives on Learning and Knowing* (2007), asks several questions that can help you think about the culturally conditioned cognitive categories of your students:

- What is the purpose of learning or going to school?
- What is the nature of knowledge? Is it passed down from one generation to the next, or is it constructed? Is there a body of knowledge to be learned? If so, where is this body of knowledge? In people' memories? Embedded in everyday life? In stories and myths? In books? Oral or written or both?
- How is this knowledge learned? Through practice, memorization, apprenticeship, formal classes?
- How is it known when one has learned? Who decides that one has learned?
- What is the role of the teacher? Who can be a teacher?
- What is the end result of learning? A better, more moral person? A wise person? An independent/ interdependent person? A knowledgable person? A better community? A more equitable society?
- What is the role of society, community, and family in learning?
- How does this perspective on learning manifest itself in your students' lives today? (pp. viii–ix)

Here are some more questions to ask that might help you get more clarity about the ways your students think about, or categorize, the world:

- How do your students think about skin color, sex, age, clothing, language, dialects, accents, or occupations?
- How might their culture affect their viewpoints about your stories, practices, or culture?

- What stereotypes exist within the group? How do they determine who is in the "in group" versus the "out group"?
- Are they more individualistic or collectivistic, and how does that affect how they approach and solve problems?
- Are they more universalistic, caring more about truth than they do relationships, or do they care more about preserving relationships than they do about the truth?
- Are they more monochronic, which means that they view time as linear and limited (and, thus, want detailed schedules and inflexible deadlines)? Or are they more polychronic, meaning that they view time as merely a tool of people (and, as such, are less concerned about schedules and deadlines)?
- How do they go about analyzing problems?
- How do they evaluate situations or behaviors?
- What are some other mental patterns you have observed?
- How do these mental patterns affect how they feel and behave? For example, do they jump to conclusions about things, or do they consider things more carefully before forming conclusions?
- How do they think about right versus wrong? What moral law do they use to differentiate between right and wrong?

5. Study Students' Motivators

What motivates your students? Studying their motivational influences can help you not only understand their behaviors but also design more effective instruction and classroom management practices.

- What gets them excited?
- What does "success" look like to them? What do they value?

- What motivates them to be or do better? To try harder?
- What do they want to achieve in life?
- What are they afraid of?
- What represents the greatest pain in their lives?
- What represents the greatest pleasure in their lives?
- What, in their view, would produce the greatest happiness in their lives?
- What would they say is the meaning or purpose of life?

6. Study Students' Goals

What are the specific goals or dreams of your students? Understanding these things can help you when it comes to capturing and keeping their attention during class, which I will discuss in more detail in the next chapter.

- What do they want to obtain or achieve?
- Who do they want to become?
- What would they like to buy or own?
- What would they like to learn?
- Where would they like to travel?
- What careers are most appealing to them?

7. Study Students' Media Influences

Most students today have been influenced by some form of media. As teachers, we must study the media influences on our students and look for ways in which they influence behavior, thought patterns, interests, and values. Seek out the answers to questions like these:

- What are their favorite movies?
- What are their favorite television or web series?
- What are their favorite cartoons?

- Who are their favorite actors and actresses?
- What kind of music do they listen to?
- Who are their favorite singers, musicians, bands, artists?
- What are their favorite songs?
- What kinds of videos do they watch on the Internet?
- What websites do they visit most frequently?
- What are some patterns of their online activity?
- What do they search for on the Internet in their leisure time?
- Do they have cell phones? Smartphones?
- How do they use their phones most frequently?
- Whom do they text the most?
- What apps do they have on their phones?
- What games do they play the most?
- Which social media do they use?
- What kinds of things do they post on social media?
- What kinds of pictures, videos, and status updates do they share on social media?

The Big Picture

A worldview is a set of beliefs, values, and presuppositions concerning life's most fundamental issues. All of us have one—including the students in our classroom. I am convinced that studying students through the seven lenses discussed can give us a fairly comprehensive sense of their worldviews. It's a way to figure out what they believe about the nature of reality, God, religion, knowledge, human beings, ethics, beauty, and politics. This is foundational insight upon which we can try to build bridges into their lives.

As a teacher, your lessons reflect, whether in explicit content or implicit assumptions, cultural patterns that either facilitate or frustrate the building of cross-cultural bridges between you and your students. The messages you communicate, whether intentionally or not, can engage or alienate students, aid or impede communication, and advance or obstruct academic and emotional growth.

It's a lesson I learned the hard way when I failed to connect with those students on the South Side of Chicago. After doing a lot of soul searching, a lot of reading, and a lot of practice being a student of those I would reach, I put together an approach that has enabled me to connect with, and teach, millions of people.

There can
be a significant
gap between where
your students are and
where you'd like them
to be. Your charge is
to bridge the divide.

4

Build Bridges

I remember walking into the gymnasium of one of the lowest-performing schools in the state. Soon it would be filled with more than 3,000 African American high school students. The district administrator who had invited me there to speak confessed that they'd never before put that many students into the gym for an assembly because they were afraid of how the students might behave.

I stood by myself along the wall, observing the students while they filed in and beginning to understand the administrator's concerns. Many of the kids were dancing, yelling, singing, and clowning around. Many of them had headphones over their ears, listening to their own music.

Their principal, a very friendly man, looked like he could have been an offensive lineman in the National Football League—nearly 7 feet tall and weighing about 350 pounds. When he got on the microphone to introduce me, he asked the audience for their attention, and they pretty much ignored him.

He tried again. "Everyone, quiet down!" he called out. "I need everyone to quiet down!" Some of the students started to comply, but the majority of the room was still filled with chatter and apathy.

If they are ignoring him—and he's their principal, and he looks like THAT—what are they going to do to me? I wondered. I began to get a little concerned, flashing back to that disastrous presentation on the South Side of Chicago.

Fortunately, this time I had done my homework. I had studied, as best as I could, the culture of these students and assessed how culturally distant I was from them. I had arrived with a plan for how I'd connect with their lives.

The principal introduced me, and maybe 14 people clapped; the rest of the 3,000 kept talking. My presentation was set to start with a video, so I dimmed the lights, but when the audience still kept talking, I had the lights turned back on. Quietly, I started to sing into the microphone. The song was "If I Can Help Somebody," a gospel standard written by A. B. Androzzo (1956) and famously recorded by the great Mahalia Jackson. *Gospel* means "good news," and the verse I chose—conveying my sincere desire to lovingly help others, cheer others, and, if necessary, gently correct others who might be "travelin' wrong" so that that my "living shall not be in vain"—was good news that I believed would make these students thirsty to hear what I had to say.

More people started to pay attention. Some started laughing. I kept a straight face, kept singing, and kept scanning my audience. I needed to take control of the room. I needed to let this group of high schoolers know that I was not scared of them and that I was on a mission. I needed to communicate to them that I cared about them enough to demand they come to order. I needed it to be clear that I had something very important for them to experience and that they ought to give me their undivided attention. I communicated all of that with only my body language, my eye contact, and how I was singing to them.

After about 30 seconds of singing, about 99 percent of the room was completely silent.

Of course, in rooms that size, in schools like that, there are always going to be some students who will test you and try to discourage you. While I was singing, there were a few kids laughing, almost uncontrollably. One young man made loud buzzer sounds to make fun of me, and that generated some laughter too. So, still singing, I started walking in his direction. Looking directly at him, I sang the line, "If I can show somebody he is travelin' wrong" and communicated with my eyes that what he was doing was not OK. That I needed him to not do it again. He got my message and sank back into his seat.

If you want to teach, you have to take loving control of your classroom. You have to establish yourself as a caring leader who is serious about the responsibility of being a teacher and who believes that to be a teacher is to be an authority worthy of respect. You need to exude an energy that says, "It's because I care that I will not allow you to take over my class." It's an attitude that should come across in how you walk, talk, teach, and lead.

That's the attitude I was exuding during that assembly. After I had complete control of the room—after I had eliminated all the "static" that would have made my job that day impossible—I had them. These teenagers gave me their undivided attention for an hour. I built a bridge into their lives that enabled us to connect on deep and meaningful levels. Afterward, hundreds of students and countless teachers and administrators told me that my assembly was one of the best, most powerful schoolwide assemblies they had ever had. A few teachers commented that they were amazed at my ability to capture and keep the attention of their students. Several administrators confessed, "Manny, you did in one hour what I have been trying to get my teachers to do in an entire year! You modeled the kind of impact they can have, the kind of difference they can make."

To teach to our potential, we must build bridges to the lives of the students we want to teach, whether we speak to 3,000 of them or 30. And we must build bridges that can take them from where they are to where we know they can be. There's a way to approach this challenge, and I'm about to share it.

Bridge Building 101

As we discussed in Chapter 3, connecting with students is only possible when we've done the work to understand their culture. Only after getting a sense of how our students *actually* think, feel, and behave should we begin focusing on what we believe our students *ought* to think, feel, or do. In addition to instilling learning habits that can help students succeed academically, I think it is equally important to teach them habits (or patterns) that can help them develop as a whole person.

For example, because many students are not learning healthy life skills at home, I believe they need to learn those things at school. As such, struggling students should be taught more than math, spelling, grammar, reading, writing, social studies, and science. They should also be taught how to cultivate a healthy self-image, self-confidence, and high moral standards. I think school leaders should teach about integrity, picking the right environments, selecting the right friends, and identifying the right mentors. Furthermore, students need to learn about goal setting, planning, and developing the habit of taking daily action to reach their goals. They need to learn about the importance of delayed gratification, budgeting, money management, conflict resolution, and social etiquette. They need to learn how to have a productive conversation and how to represent themselves online (via social media). They might also need to learn about personal hygiene and other things that they may have not learned at home. Attending to these kinds of things in schools can produce a much richer, broader set of outcomes for our students than academic success alone.

As the diagram on page 70 illustrates, there can be a significant gap between where your students are and where you'd like them to be. Your charge is to bridge the divide.

The challenge is to help students grow beyond their current patterns of thinking, feeling, and behaving to embrace the patterns of thinking, feeling, and behaving that can help them flourish in every area of their lives.

The Critical Gap

Our understanding of what students think, feel, and do right now.

Context

What we would like students to think, feel, and do.

Content

From Goals to Growth

The first step is to be clear about the objectives for each lesson you are trying to teach. I believe it's as simple as getting into the habit of saying to yourself, "As a result of this lesson, I want my students to learn *what?* I want my students to feel *what?* I want my students to do (or be able to do) *what?*" Think through these questions until you can provide very specific answers.

For example, do you want them to feel something about a topic? Do you want them to feel a sense of wonder at the intricacies of mathematics? A sense of responsibility for the environment? Compassion for Romeo and Juliet? Love for their fellow human beings? Intolerance for injustice or frustration with obstacles to political change? Curiosity about how numbers on a screen translate into video games? What would you like them to feel?

Teachers are used to thinking about what students should be able to do as a result of the lessons they deliver; this is the foundation of standards-based instruction. When you are pinpointing what you would like your students to know or learn how to do as a result of each lesson, certainly think about academic outcomes, but think beyond them, too. Maybe you want your students to get better at adding and subtracting fractions or incorporating supporting evidence into persuasive essays. But maybe you also want them to make some changes in their behavior—participate more in class conversation, check their work before they turn it in, or treat their classmates with courtesy and respect. Figure out what you want students to do, be precise in naming it, and target your instruction to support their progress toward those ends.

Lev Vygotsky's zone of proximal development (ZPD) theory (1978) comes to our aid when thinking about the kinds of objectives we create for our students. The ZPD is a descriptive term for the area between the student's current developmental level "as determined by independent problem solving" and the level of development that the student could achieve "through adult guidance or in collaboration with more capable peers" (p. 84ff). Vygotsky argued that teaching should take place in the ZPD, the cognitive space between the boring and the improbable. In that space, with scaffolding or support from teacher or peers, individuals can find the right degree of challenge to spur learning.

Vygotsky's theory reminds us that each child has a unique timetable of cognitive development—that each child's ZPD is different. When we cultivate relationships with our students, we gain insight into the most developmentally appropriate objectives for each. Knowing who students are, where they come from, and what they think, feel, and believe adds critical missing dimensions to transcripts and sets of test scores.

Only after we have become a student of our students, and have created developmentally appropriate objectives to help them grow, can we begin to bridge the divide between their contexts and our content.

Connecting Our Content to Their Context

The next step is to create lesson plans that intentionally and thoughtfully connect our content—what we want students to think, feel, and do—to their context. This is the only way to capture and keep their attention and to enlist their participation in learning.

To build a bridge, you must seek to identify some aspect of the student's language or culture that is related to your subject matter. Linguists who translate books from one language to another refer to this process as "functional equivalence" or "dynamic equivalence." This is a translation method that focuses on capturing the thought or idea of the writer as accurately as possible rather than replicating the writer's exact forms and words. It's about conveying meaning, not just finding dictionary-equivalent words.

Teachers must seek to do the same thing: find and use functional equivalents in the lessons we teach. We need to understand the content (thoughts, ideas, understandings, outcomes) that we intend to teach our students, and then we need to translate that content so it is understandable in their words and within their culture. And to do that, we leverage what we've learned through our seven-part curricular study of who our students are and where they come from, including their social structures and interactions, their language, their mindset and motivators, their goals, and the media they value. This is how we give our students the instruction they need. This is how we create understanding. Connecting our content and their context, via the kinds of links shown in the diagram below, is our only hope of getting students to grasp and care about the objectives we set. And it's our best hope for helping them grow mentally, emotionally, and behaviorally.

The Instruction Students Need

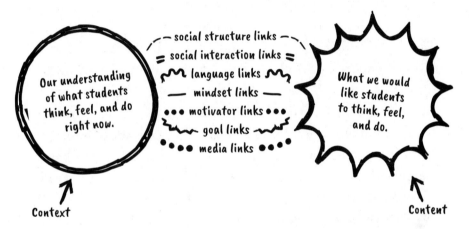

Here's an example. If I wanted to teach students about grammar, I would consider their cultural backgrounds and try to find examples from their cultures to make the lessons more relevant. That's actually what one of my favorite teachers did in my high school English class. She dissected the works of Tupac Shakur, Biggie Smalls, Nas, and Snoop Doggy Dogg to teach us grammar—nouns, verbs, and adjectives; subjects and predicates; independent and dependent clauses. Now, if I wanted to teach grammar today to African American students on the South Side of Chicago, I would first need to recognize that their cultural context is a little different from mine, even though I am black too. Their heroes are different, for example. So it would not be wise for me to try to use Tupac, Snoop, Biggie, or Nas to engage them. Rather, I might diagram lyrics from one of their favorite rappers or singers (using the radio versions of songs rather than the explicit versions) or dialogue spoken by their favorite movie stars. And because who they admire will be changing frequently, I would need to constantly be studying their culture in order to remain as close to their world as possible.

Furthermore, if I were trying to teach grammar to white students in a rural area, I would have a different content-to-context divide to bridge, but would similarly seek functional equivalents, following the same pattern of examining social structure, behavior patterns, symbols, objects, artifacts, rituals, greetings, events, activities, language, slang, phrases, media influences, and whatever else they care about in order to capture and keep their attention. I'd probably still have some hip-hop lyrics in these grammar lessons, but there would be country music and rock lyrics, too.

The bridge-building process is not a one-time, one-way connection. It requires us to go back and forth, continually creating new spans linking context to content, showing students the relationship between the two. Continually alternating between their context and your content is the way to build the sturdiest and longest-lasting bridge.

Teaching That Changes Lives

This kind of teaching, with clear goals translated into functional equivalents that I could actually understand, is what kept me awake in class and provoked me to ask questions. It inspired and challenged me, and pushed me to think more critically. This kind of teaching, which targets and resonates with your particular, idiosyncratic students, will make them look forward to coming to your class. A bridge, once it's built, allows for movement both ways. When you meet students in the middle, you're positioned to make your goals their goals, and they're positioned to use what they're learning to chart a new destiny.

Self-concept is a
world changer.

5

Give Them Glimpses of Their Own Possibilities

When I was in high school, a substitute history teacher played a video that changed my life. It was a recording of the Reverend Dr. Martin Luther King, Jr.'s "I Have a Dream" speech. Delivered in 1963 on the steps of the Lincoln Memorial, this speech injected hope into the veins of marginalized Americans—including me, several decades later. Dr. King's words were a reminder that the United States government, which for more than 100 years had officially denied its black citizens the right to life, liberty, and the freedom to pursue happiness, had done very little apart from signing pieces of paper to help black people stand on their own two feet, politically and economically.

When Dr. King delivered that speech, many black Americans were still unable to vote. They were the last hired and the first fired. They were receiving the least amount of resources for the education of their children, and it was illegal for them to integrate public facilities, like bus stations or restaurants. To protest those injustices, Dr. King raised his voice that day to call our nation to turn the page. He used the power of his own voice to paint a poignant picture of what our planet could become if all people were treated with dignity and respect. Sitting in my high school classroom, I got goosebumps listening to that speech. Something inside of me changed.

It was on that day, after that class, that I had the first realization that I, too, could use my voice and my life for a noble purpose. I began seeing visions of myself standing before groups of people, inspiring them with my words. In fact, visions of speaking to groups became so frequent that when I heard other speakers make presentations during assemblies, I often saw flashes of myself standing in their place, delivering my own speech.

That video of Dr. King, a man who looked like me, gave me a glimpse of my own possibilities. It planted into my soul a seed of hope, that I too could make a difference in the world. When you show your students examples of successful, useful, fulfilled people who look like them, you show them what is possible for their own lives.

The Construction of Destiny

I have learned that exposure is the birthplace of big dreams and motivation. If you want your students to do more, they have to see more and then commit to be more. From that, they will do more.

I don't believe most unsuccessful students are lazy, but I do believe that they have not been exposed to anything that has inspired them. They have not been put in situations where they could see what they might do and become, or they are so distracted by other priorities or traumatic circumstances that they cannot see hope at all. We cannot solve all our students' problems, but we can work hard to open their eyes and help them see themselves in a different light. Although we have little influence on many of the challenges they face, we do have influence over their self-concept, and that's a tremendous power to have.

Self-concept is a world changer. Consider that how you see yourself influences how you think, how you feel, and how you behave. So if you want to expand your possibilities, you must expand your sense of your own capabilities. You must adapt new beliefs about who you are and what you can do.

In the diagram on page 82, I lay out my understanding of how a person can change his or her life. It reflects my belief that destiny is something we construct ourselves through our daily habits (or behaviors). These habits are built upon our individual actions, and our actions are based upon our decisions or our choices. Our choices are influenced by our emotional state, and our emotional state reflects what we believe to be fundamentally true about ourselves.

The Change Process

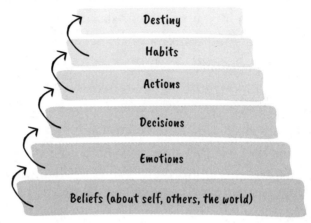

Change

To you, I say this: As a teacher, as an adult in a kid's life, you can have a tremendous impact at every stage of this process. If you help your students change their beliefs about themselves, this will change their emotional states. If you help them change their emotional states, this will allow them to make better choices. If you help them make better choices, this will allow them to take more proactive steps to improve their lives. If you help them continue down the path of better choices, they will develop the habits that allow for a better quality of life and improve their destiny. I am absolutely convinced that if you want to change the lives of your students, you must begin by helping them change their beliefs.

Here's the obvious question: "If changing the beliefs of my students is so fundamental to their destinies, then how do I help change their beliefs?" I thought you'd never ask!

New References

First, I think we need to establish a common understanding of what beliefs are and how they function. For a working definition, let's use this: *A belief is a feeling within us that something corresponds to reality—that something is true.*

Where did your beliefs come from? How did you get them? Why do you still have them, or how have they changed? I'm convinced that beliefs grow out of our experiences. Things we have been through in our lives lead us to adopt feelings of certainty about various aspects of ourselves and the world around us. If something happens to you over and over again, eventually you form a pattern in your head that this is the way life is. I consider these formative experiences to be "references." As illustrated below, the more references you have for a belief, the stronger it is.

The Foundation of Our Beliefs

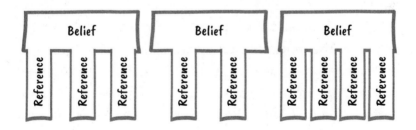

For example, if I were a student, and I had never seen anyone in my family graduate from high school (reference), then it's not that difficult to conclude that I probably wouldn't expect to graduate from high school either (belief). Or if I had never done well on my tests or my quizzes (reference), then it's not that hard to see why I'd consider myself stupid (belief). Or if all of the men in my family were unfaithful to their partners (reference), then you'd understand why I'd conclude that men are incapable of monogamy (belief).

Our students' destinies, by which I mean *the quality of their lives,* are grounded in their beliefs, and their beliefs are based upon their references. The answer is to provide our students with better references. Show them that their reality is only a sliver of the vast reality that lies beyond what they have seen and known. If we want them to be more, then they must see more. They must be exposed to more. They must see *what else* is possible.

Helen Keller realized this. She was born blind and deaf; reality for her was dark and silent. But once she realized there was more beyond, she pursued it with fierce tenacity, unwavering determination, and unrelenting vigor. She learned to communicate, to read, and to write—not just passably, but very well. Reflecting on her own circumstances and the obstacles she had overcome, Keller concluded, "Worse than being blind is to see but have no vision."

Most of our students can see, but too many of them have no vision. They have not glimpsed their own possibilities. And this being so, too many of them are apathetic about school and mediocre achievers or worse. They cannot see what they could become, driven by their very well-referenced and yet tragically constricted beliefs about themselves and the world. Their low self-esteem and poor self-concept feed emotional reactions, bad decisions, self-sabotaging actions, destructive habits, and an unsatisfying life.

That is why I believe one of the most important jobs of teachers to expose students to *more.* It's to expose them to the world beyond the world they know, and to plant dreams that grow into mental pictures of success—visions of what they are not yet but could become. Kids who are being exposed to just rapping, rebounding, or robbing, or who have other, equally limited models of what success looks like, need to see what else is out there.

Let me tell you how this has worked in my life. When I was in high school, my English teacher Erin Gruwell encouraged me to apply to college. However, because no one in my family had ever graduated from high school, I did not believe that I was college material. She argued with me, but her telling me I was underestimating myself did not really change my mind.

What Ms. G did next was drive me and my classmates to the Claremont Colleges in Southern California and arrange a college tour for us. We walked around campus, sat in lectures, toured academic buildings, and visited with coaches. Toward the end of the tour, we had lunch with a group of college students. At my table were several undergraduates, all of them white. Although they were very kind and encouraging, I felt so intimidated. I did not believe that I was smart enough to be among college students, who had to be so much smarter than I was. I didn't want to open my mouth in case I said something stupid and confirmed it. Then, one of the college students at the table, a guy who had not spoken very much, started talking. I don't remember what he talked about, but I remember being surprised that he didn't sound any smarter than I considered myself to be. A light bulb went on in my head: *If he's in college, and I'm at least as smart as he is, then maybe I can go to college too!* That experience on that college campus that day, that reference, changed how I saw myself.

It helped to change my self-concept and my idea of what was possible for my future.

That same high school teacher once took my classmates and me to dinner at a nice restaurant—the kind where you'll find place settings with three forks, two spoons, three plates, and a whole lot of other stuff. At the time, I was so uncomfortable being there. The other people in the restaurant were dressed very nicely, and I was wearing blue jeans, tennis shoes, and a T-shirt. I felt out of place. I didn't know which fork to use first, and I didn't know what to do with my napkin.

Ms. G encouraged us to just relax and enjoy ourselves. After I was able to calm down, I started looking around at the other people in the restaurant. One table caught my attention. At the table was a man, a woman, and three children. It was a father, a mother, and their kids. They were a beautiful family. They were so beautiful, in fact, that I couldn't stop staring at them. They looked like they were enjoying one another, laughing and talking to each other. That family looked like it was filled with love. I became somewhat emotional, but I wasn't quite sure why. After reflecting for a moment, it hit me that I had never seen a father eat dinner with his family like that. Most of the men in my family abandoned us and our mothers. Right then, I said in my heart, *I want to have a family just like that.* This experience was another critical reference for me, the foundation for a new belief in what was possible, a picture of the kind of family that I might have. I do not believe in coincidence, and I find it interesting that today, my wife and I have three beautiful children.

What can you expose your students to in order to inspire them, giving them glimpses of their own possibilities? If you are working with kids who are despondent or disinterested, you might want to expose them to new things through field trips. You might even want to do so in smaller groups. The more challenging the child, the more attention that child will need. Maybe you're in a position to do what my teacher did for me—take a handful of students to a college campus. It can go a long way in opening their hearts and minds to you. Maybe, as it did for me, it will even expand their self-concept.

I've met young people in almost every major city in the United States, and many of them have never left the neighborhoods in which they were born. I have met young people who live on the South Side of Chicago who have never been to the Loop or the Magnificent Mile. Growing up in Long Beach, I had never been to downtown Los Angeles, even though it was less than 30 miles away.

It took a teacher to expose me to more than rapping, rebounding, and robbing. It took a teacher to take me to a college campus in order to help me see that college was a possibility for me, that I was college material. It took a teacher to take me to nicer restaurants to help me see that I too could one day have a happy, healthy family. She exposed us to more, and that exposure helped us want more, and inspired us to work harder.

Whatever you decide to do, please don't underestimate your power to provide experiences that could literally change your students' lives.

One of the most powerful things you can do as a teacher is show students how to process their experiences through writing.

6

Help Them Find Their Voices

Every one of you has a voice, and I am going to help you find it, because the world needs to hear it. So I want you to pick up these journals, and I want you to write. I want you to write about that time you lost your friend who was mowed down in a drive-by shooting; write about the time you lost your innocence to your pedophile uncle; and write about that time you were thrown off a balcony for trying to protect your mother, and you were just a little boy. Write from your heart. Just get it out. We'll deal with grammar and syntax later.

Those were the words I remember Ms. G. using to encourage us to begin journaling. It was a defining moment for our class, because no teacher had ever given us the freedom to write about our lives like that.

When Ms. G entered our class on her first day as a teacher, she was clueless about us. Despite all her cheerleader alacrity (acquired growing up in a gated community in affluent Orange County, California); despite the repertoire of instructional best practices taught to her by her graduate school professors; despite her very thorough syllabus, which had printed on it the names of some great writers such as Chaucer, Hemingway, and Frost, Ms. G had no idea how to teach us—her socioeconomically challenged, very multicultural class.

Most of us felt like we were living in a war zone. That year alone in Long Beach, California, more than 100 teenagers were killed by gang violence. Some of them were our friends. Every day, we wondered if we would be the next victim. And this was only one of the threats that had us on alert. It was not uncommon for fights to break out or shootings to take place at sporting events, skating rinks, house parties, or even on the way to and from school.

I remember walking home from school one evening and having a carful of gang members pull up alongside and point their guns at me. There was nowhere to run, no way to get away from them, so I just stood there helplessly, paralyzed, as they ran the red targeting lasers of their guns over my chest and face. For reasons that elude me, they pulled off abruptly, tires screeching as they drove away. I lived to see another day.

Another night, I was walking home after a football game, and a car started following me. To get away from it, I jumped fences and cut through people's yards, waiting it out in the dark until it seemed safe. A little while later, the car found me again, and when I started sprinting to get away, I heard the shooting start. I dove over another fence and crawled to safety, absolutely terrified for my life. The car sped off. Another day survived.

This was the way of things in Long Beach at the time, and I honestly did not believe that I would live to see my 18th birthday. I just knew that sooner or later, I would be killed for being in the wrong place at the wrong time, even if I was minding my own business. I was not the only one who felt that way. Most of my classmates feared for their lives, too.

Things were often just as discouraging at home. Almost everyone in our class was being raised by a single parent or grandparent and dealing with feelings of parental abandonment. Most of us had one or both parents addicted to drugs or alcohol. All of us had at least one family member who was incarcerated. Most of us had lost a friend to gang violence. I do not think it is unreasonable to assert that many kids who grew up in my neighborhood and ones like it were suffering from some of kind of post-traumatic stress disorder. Unlike soldiers returning from the battlefield, few of us ever received counseling for the trauma we experienced. We were just expected to keep functioning in school and life. To just get over it. To pull ourselves together and show "grit." This would not be expected of traumatized soldiers, and it should not be expected of traumatized youth.

Many kids who have experienced great hardship need a place to "get some things out." They need a space to express their pain, their problems, their tragedies, and their trauma. They need teachers and counselors who are comfortable with being made uncomfortable by their students' very harsh realities. Students needs teachers who give them the freedom to heal. Because of that, one of the most powerful things you can do as a teacher is show students how to process their experiences through writing. By encouraging them to write their truth, you can help them find their own voices and experience their own power.

Exposure to Models and Inspiration

Getting traumatized, disconnected, or otherwise unenthusiastic students to write in an honest, expressive, and illuminating way is easier said than done, of course. This is an area where giving students glimpses of their own possibilities is particularly important. As we discussed in Chapter 5, the way to do that is through exposure. Students who don't know how to process and express themselves constructively need models to follow—a wide variety of speakers, writers, and artists with whom they can identify, who come from a neighborhood similar to their own, and who have faced obstacles similar to the ones they themselves are facing. Experiencing these voices lets students hear what their own voices could sound like. It validates their experiences as significant and worthy of attention.

Guest Speakers

For nearly 20 years, I have been telling people my story because I want them to see that they too can overcome some of the obstacles in their own lives. Tens of thousands of people have approached to thank me for telling my story . . . and for telling theirs in the process.

That's the point I want to stress. When you bring relatable guest speakers into your classroom or school, you give students a sense of the significance of their own experiences and of what their own voices might sound like. I recommend emphasizing this parallel by following up guest speakers with journaling or writing exercises. The speaker telling his or her story can serve as a jumping-off point for students telling theirs.

Memoirs and Autobiographies

Similarly, exposing your students to memoirs and autobiographies can be tremendously helpful when trying to help them find their own voices. When I was younger, teachers introduced me to autobiographies of Malcolm X and Frederick Douglass, two authors who had a huge impact on my own development. I was so inspired by their tenacity to learn how to read and write that I could not put down their books.

Their words awakened in me a fire to learn more. I began to read stories by and about the Reverend Dr. Martin Luther King, Jr., and the Montgomery Bus Boycott. I read about Rosa Parks and the Montgomery Improvement Association. I read the stories of the people who participated in the Albany Movement, the Birmingham Movement, and the March from Selma to Montgomery. I was beyond inspired by Dr. King's *Letter from Birmingham Jail* and the beauty and power with which he expressed himself. I mourned the four little girls who were murdered in the bombing of the 16th Street Baptist Church. I wept over the murders of civil rights activists Viola Liuzzo, Mickey Schwerner, Andrew Goodman, and James Chaney. In my mind, I journeyed with the Black Panthers, Stokely Carmichael, the Student Nonviolent Coordinating Committee, the Urban

League, and the NAACP; I joined the 1963 March on Washington, walked the picket lines in the Memphis sanitation strike of 1968, and enlisted in the War on Poverty, in which people from all over the country occupied our nation's capital for poor people everywhere. I felt that all these stories were also, in some way, related to my own story. When I read about these events, my soul somehow felt validated and empowered.

So I drank deeply from memoirs and autobiographies from this era of history, and I wrestled with their ideas about justice, sacrifice, and service. Those books spoke for me in a way that I had never before heard. They inspired me to change my role models from athletes to people who dedicated their lives to helping others in need. (Other than Muhammad Ali, Jim Brown, and Kareem Abdul Jabbar, I didn't see any athletes standing for the least, the last, the lost, or the left out.) Where kids put up posters of sports stars, musicians, entertainers, I put up pictures of Dr. King with his family, Malcolm X and his family, and Nelson Mandela. I looked at these photos whenever I needed to be reminded of what really mattered or to make the most of my opportunity for a college education, which their work had made possible.

The more I read the writing of people who participated in the U.S. Civil Rights Movement, the more indebted I felt to them. I started to emulate them in how I wrote, and eventually, in how I spoke to people. It is completely accurate to say that their writing helped me find my voice and, ultimately, inspired me to use my voice for the voiceless.

Exposure to memoirs, autobiographies, and documentaries that capture the words of admirable figures can have the same effect on the students you teach. The resources you choose don't have to be the ones my teachers introduced to me, but they should be written by or about people with whom your particular students can identify. Whether your students are white, black, Latino, Native American, or Asian, and whether they are living in urban areas or rural ones, there are stories out there that will give voice to some of their experiences and model constructive responses to the challenges they face.

Musicians and Musical Artists

Artists are artists because they can express truth in profound and transformative ways. Musicians, in particular, communicate in a manner that hits us at the very core of our being. Because of that, I advise teachers who are looking to help students develop their voices to bring the work of singers, rappers, and other musicians into the classroom.

If your students love rap or hip-hop music, encourage them to write their own raps. If they love country music, have them compose lyrics to their own songs. If they love punk rock or heavy metal or any other genre of music that has lyrics, encourage them to dissect the lyrics of their favorite songs and describe why these words affect them so powerfully. Getting students to write about their favorite artists and songs is a great way to help them find their voices while also addressing instructional goals related to grammar and syntax.

The Imitation Approach

In Ancient Greece, students of rhetoric were required to memorize and deliver the speeches of famous orators. Once they gained facility with this, they crafted original speeches that imitated the style of those orators. This imitation model—having students mimic the speaking or writing styles of people or artists they admire—is still useful for teachers today. Some might raise an eyebrow at this old-fashioned approach, but I have learned that imitation can be a very helpful precursor to originality. It's through trying on different voices that students develop an authentic one of their own.

There are all kinds of ways to go about this. Provide models and then have students write (and perform, as appropriate) a journal entry, speech, story, poem, essay, or song that imitates another creator's style. Encourage them to use similar grammar and syntax. Have them use metaphors and similes, personification, anaphora, epistrophe, parataxis, climaxes, and other tropes and figures that their models use. Sometimes choose the models yourself, as part of your efforts to expose students to a wide variety of voices, and sometimes allow students to choose their own models and imitate their favorites.

Don't forget to work with students to identify and explain the parallels between their imitations and the originals. Awareness of the artist's technique can open our eyes to the possibility of our own artistry. It's not magic, how our favorite writers or speakers express themselves; it's mastery. They have devoted themselves and mastered their craft. Students have their own authentic experiences to share, and these experiences are worth hearing. With the addition of working to become masters of their craft, they can refine their voice into one that has a particular impact . . . into one that others will listen *for* and listen *to*.

Self-Expression for Healing and Empowerment

Ms. G used to have us write in our journals almost every day. She would give us topics, but then step back so that we could express ourselves. Sometimes she would ask us to write about the happiest and saddest moments of our lives. Or she would ask us to describe our families, describe our neighborhoods, and describe our hopes and dreams and our biggest fears. Sometimes Ms. G asked us to write about people who inspired us and to explain why, or to share our opinions on recent events or controversial topics. By encouraging us to write, and giving us the freedom to do so without judgment, she helped many of us find our own voice.

For some of my classmates, Ms. G provided a window into great literature; for me, she parted the curtains and she let the sun shine in. She helped me appreciate the beauty of the English language and laid the foundation for me to learn how to make language sing and sting. By giving me the space to air my pain and my problems, my hopes and my dreams, she helped me learn how to use words to pierce, prod, and empower. Journaling helped me find the words to express pride in myself and in my culture. Journaling even helped me to heal. To this day, after all these years, I still journal. In fact, I have stacks of journals locked away in a safe place. They are filled with tears, trauma, healing, and hope. My journals have been my counselors. In no small way, those journals have helped me find, refine, and strengthen the person I am.

In today's schools, writing is no longer restricted to English classes. Therefore, I encourage you, whatever subject or grade level you teach, to incorporate journaling into your instruction as a way to help students not just reflect on content but also reflect on themselves. Teach them to summon the English language and send it forth into battle. Teach them that the pen is mightier than the sword. Teach them that their experiences, their opinions, their voices matter. Teach them to use their voices to connect, to help, and to heal.

Students who
doubt themselves
are locked in a battle
with their most
formidable foe.

7

Believe in Them Until
They Believe in Themselves

After reading my journal entries and observing the way I carried myself, Ms. G. pulled me aside one day and said, "Manny, you have to go to college. Do you want to go to college?"

"Thank you," I replied, "but no one in my family even graduated from high school." I was flattered, but at the same time, what she said sounded crazy. College wasn't for people like me.

Ms. G looked a little bothered by my reply. Then she said something like, "I didn't become a teacher because of where you are from but because of where you could go. Manny," she insisted, "you can go to college."

"But I'm not college material," I said in defeat.

"Sure you are, Manny. Sure you are!" She started talking about how college could help me do some of the things I'd said I wanted to do: help my mom financially, travel the world, and help more people who were in need.

"I'll help you, Manny," Ms. G continued, "but only if you let me. You have to be willing to work for it."

Because my family used to live by some Air Force bases in Colorado, I had always seen myself becoming a pilot. So when my teacher was encouraging me to go to college, I was still wrestling with the idea of enlisting in the Air Force. Ms. G stressed that I could always go into the Air Force *after* I finished college. Still, I shrugged off her advice.

Then one night, after some of my friends and I had been out playing basketball with Ms. G's husband and his friends, we went over to her apartment, where there was a stack of college applications on the dining room table. She asked me to look through the stack and pull out applications of the schools that interested me. As I leafed through, I saw applications to Harvard, Yale, Columbia, NYU, San Diego State, and many others.

"Where do you want to go?" my teacher asked me, with an excited smile on her face.

"I don't know," I answered. You see, although I am now familiar with all those schools, back then, none of their names meant anything to me. I had no idea what Harvard or

Yale was. I had no idea what NYU or Columbia was. I was a little embarrassed by this, actually. So I turned the question on her: "Where do *you* think I should apply to college?"

Her eyes lit up, and she said, "Why don't you to apply to my dream school, UC Berkeley? It's the Harvard of the West Coast—like the Ivy League. I had a 4.2 GPA, and they didn't let me in," she continued. "But you, Manny, you had 0.6 and were a high school dropout, and now you're back. You were a terrible student, and now your GPA is about 3.9. Manny, they might see your potential!" She was always so enthusiastic and hopeful.

All that sounded nice but, like I said, I had no idea what Harvard or the Ivy League was. "Where is it, Ms. G?"

She told me UC Berkeley was by San Francisco. I didn't know where that was either, and maybe it showed on my face.

"It's in the Bay Area," she continued.

"Is that around here? Is it in California?" I asked.

Then, perhaps trying to draw on her knowledge of African American culture, she said, "It's where Jason Kidd plays basketball."

Now, that sealed the deal for me, but not for reasons you might expect. You see, I was never really a basketball fan. I was more of a football guy. But the way Ms. G said "Jason Kidd" touched something in my heart. The emotion in her voice, the look in her eyes, that intense *hope* for me. *Why does this lady seem to care so much about my future?* I wondered. *Why does she seem to care more about my future than I do? I can't do anything for her, and she wants nothing from me in return. I don't understand it.* All these thoughts were bouncing around in my head and heart. But then I said to myself, *If this guy named Jason Kidd and this place called UC Berkeley are so important to her, then Manny, the least you can do is act like you care about those things.* With a smile on my face, I said, "Yeah, that's where I want to go."

I'll never forget the day I received an acceptance package from UC Berkeley. When I showed it to Ms. G, she started jumping up and down in front of her freshman class, and then she started to cry.

The lesson here is that sometimes you have to believe in someone else's belief in you until your own belief is born. Ms. G believed in me academically before I believed in myself. I honestly didn't think any college would accept me, but she did. She believed for me. She saw my potential, gave me a glimpse of it, and kept calling me up to it. She refused to let me, or others, settle for mediocrity. She challenged us to dream bigger and to work harder, to make more out of our lives.

You can do the same for your students. If you recall from Chapter 5, belief is the basis upon which everyone's emotions, decisions, actions, and habits are built. It is the stream from which our destiny flows. By believing in your students, you can become a reference point for them that changes how they see themselves.

The Power of Belief

Do you believe in your students? Do you believe that they are greater than their circumstances? Do you believe that teaching them has less to do with where they are from and more to do with where they could go?

It is true that students rise or fall to our level of expectations for them. If you do not really believe in your students, then you won't have ambitious expectations for them. It's not that it would be acceptable for them to fail, exactly, but maybe you'll lower your standards to something "more realistic," which means allowing them to remain average or mediocre. But the glorious opposite is also true: Your faith in students plants a seed that can grow into their faith in themselves. By believing in their possibility and making that belief known, you can empower them to transcend many of the obstacles in their lives. Your impenetrable belief in your students can be the fuel that launches them into greatness.

One day, after I had delivered a speech at a high school in Pennsylvania, a young lady approached me. She was tall, with dark hair and brown skin and a shining round face. I greeted her by giving her a hug. "Hello, beautiful," I said. "How are you?"

The young lady shook her head and said, "No."

I was confused. "No, what?" I asked. "What do you mean?"

"Don't call me beautiful," she replied.

"But you are beautiful."

She shook her head again "No. No. No, I'm not. I'm not beautiful."

My confusion turned to concern. "What do you mean? Sure, you're beautiful. Why don't you think so?"

She started crying. "No one has ever called me that," she said.

"You mean to tell me no one in your life has ever told you that you are beautiful—not even your parents?" I asked.

"No. You're the first person who has *ever* called me that. I'm not beautiful. People have always called me fat, and ugly. No one has ever told me that they think I'm beautiful."

I spent the next 30 minutes trying to help that young lady change her self-image.

Some of your students might have similar beliefs that are limiting them, holding them back, and robbing them of realizing their potential. I have heard others refer to these kinds of self-sabotaging beliefs as "stinkin' thinkin'," and that's a good description. As a teacher, one of your primary objectives should be to identify these harmful beliefs and target them not just for elimination but for replacement with something better.

Teaching the Power of the Self

Students who doubt themselves are locked in a battle with their most formidable foe. Certainly one of the hardest things I've ever done in life is believe in myself, and believe that I could achieve my dreams if I really worked hard.

If your students are ever going to flourish in school, work, or life, they are going to need a healthy self-image. How they see themselves is foundational to everything they think, say, feel, and do. Their thoughts about themselves determine almost everything else in their lives.

One of my favorite poems, attributed to Walter Wintle and published back in the early 1900s, shares some essential truths:

> *If you think you are beaten, you are*
> *If you think you dare not, you don't,*
> *If you like to win, but you think you can't*
> *It is almost a certain you won't.*

If you think you'll lose, you're lost
For out of the world we find,
Success begins with a fellow's will
It's all in the state of mind.

If you think you are outclassed, you are
You've got to think high to rise.
You've got to be sure of yourself before
You can ever win a prize.

Life's battles don't always go
To the stronger or faster man,
But soon or late the man who wins
Is the man who thinks he can!

It is indeed true that the man who thinks he can and the man who thinks he can't are both right. Your students' belief in themselves is essential to their success, and you have the power to help them believe that they are smart enough, strong enough, and capable enough to make their dreams a reality. It's true that each student fights his or her own battle for self-respect and self-confidence, but you, as a teacher, can help equip them for success.

Although your students might come from very humble neighborhoods and families, you must continually remind them that they are somebody, that they are valuable, that they matter. Just because your students live in an undesirable place doesn't mean that the negative, depressing, destructive conditions of that place have to live in them. Your belief in them can help them see that they can define situations rather than letting their situations define them. Help them see that their worth is intrinsic, not tied to circumstance. Reinforce to them that they are created with infinite beauty, worth, value, and purpose.

Teach them that *they* control how they see themselves—not other people. Teach them that when they *make* a mistake, it does not mean that *they* are a mistake. Teach them that just because they have failed at something, it does not mean that *they* are failures. Teach them that they are greater than their shortcomings and greater than their mistakes. They are greater than their lack of education, greater than poverty, greater than racism.

As a teacher, you are in a prime position to help students realize that they are the drivers of their own lives and destinies, and that they already have the most important thing they need: the power to focus their minds and hearts on their dreams and make those dreams a reality.

Teach them that they have been blessed with this power, but in order to activate it, they have to put it to use. The dreams they have conceived in their heads and hearts must be married to their belief in themselves. To survive and thrive in life, they must believe. They must believe that they are enough. They must believe that they are able. They must believe that they are powerful. Only then can their lives improve and their dreams be achieved.

But they need you to go first. Teacher, *believe*.

Yes, there are going
to be times when
you feel like a failure.
During those times,
remember these words:
Don't give up, *get up*.

8

Keep Showing Up

The day had finally come. Standing on the stage at the University of California at Berkeley's Hearst Greek Theater in my cap and gown, waiting to receive my degree, I looked out at the nearly 9,000 people from all over the world who had gathered to celebrate our graduation. They were dressed to impress in their Sunday best. It was like a vibrant worship service at a black church, and the entire audience in the theater became the choir, singing and praising, clapping and swaying, uniting their spirits with the music that was blasting through the speakers:

Take the shackles off my feet so I can dance
I just want to praise you
I just want to praise you
You broke the chains now I can lift my hands
And I'm gonna praise you
I'm gonna praise you

We turned Berkeley, the paragon of protest, into the apotheosis of praise. Maybe the gaiety and merriment was so full because many of our journeys had been so hard. Joy that has known no sorrow is no joy at all, for it is only through deep and personal intimacy with great grief that our hearts can fully experience great joy.

My joy was like a cup overflowing. Breathing hard upon my remembrance were all the doubts and discouragements, all the dejection and despair, all the homeless shelters, all the dumpsters, all the alcohol, all the drugs, all the fights, all the abuse, all the blood, and all the death and the pain and the tears that I had endured.

Then they called my name.

I walked proudly across the stage and received my degree, becoming the first person in my family to graduate from college. I made it. I should have been addicted to drugs, but I made it. I should have been locked up, but I made it. I should have been dead, but I made it. I made it through the dark days. I made it through the starless nights. I made it!

After they handed me my degree, I took just a moment to gaze over the sea of celebration and really take in the fullness of the experience. There in the audience, I saw her face. I wasn't sure she was going to be able to make it, but she did. It was Momma. Our eyes met. She was sitting by herself between two well-dressed families who looked like they had been to a few college graduations. Unable to contain her emotion, tears began rolling down Momma's face. Dabbing at her tears with a piece of tissue, she mouthed, "I love you."

As soon as the ceremony was over, I jumped off the stage, ran to her, and gave her the biggest hug. There wasn't any better way to say just how much that day meant to both of us.

As we reach the end of this book, I hope that it has reminded you of the incredible power of love and service. Today I am who I am, and I am where I am, not only because I have worked hard to improve my life. My destiny was created by me, but it was steered by people who came into my life and helped me. I seriously doubt that I would be where I am had it not been for the man who sat next to me on a park bench, on a day when I was a dropout drowning in despair, and encouraged me to go back to high school; for the teachers who believed in me; for the coaches who pushed me; or for the school secretaries, janitors, lunch ladies, librarians, and many others who went out of their way to encourage me, support me, confront me. These people gave their time and their resources to give me hope and practical help. They didn't have great financial resources, but they had hearts full of love. They were just ordinary folks, with their own challenges to face, but they were heroes too, and they did extraordinary work that prepared me to meet my challenges and thrive in this world.

The teachers who steered me lived and taught in a way that made me thirsty for an education. They were students of their students, and they built culturally relevant bridges into our lives, and from our lives to the goals they set for us. They gave us glimpses of our own possibilities, and they believed in us until we believed in ourselves. When they failed, they learned from their mistakes and kept showing up. For them, I am so thankful. I am thankful to have been touched by their kindness and love. I am grateful to have been blessed by each and every one of them.

I hope you see that you too have the power to make a positive difference in the lives of your students. I hope you see that who you are, right now, is enough—enough to change a life, enough to give someone hope, and enough to give someone help. On your worst day, you might be a student's best hope. On your worst day, you might be a kid's last chance.

Persist and Learn

Now sure, there are going to be times when you blow it. There are going to be times when your attempt to build a bridge into your students' lives does not work as effectively as you had hoped or even blows up entirely. There are going to be times when the field trip you arranged did not have the kind of impact you wanted it to have. Yes, there are going to be times when you feel like a failure. During those times, remember these words: Don't give up, *get up*. Learn from your mistakes. Try something else. Keep showing up, keep putting in the work.

A lot of what Ms. G learned was by trial and error. I remember a time in our class when nothing she tried was working. Kids would argue with her or just ignore her. I remember looking at her from my spot in the back of the classroom and thinking, *Yeah, she's going quit pretty soon. She seems nice, but she is about to give up. Good try, lady.* But then, the next day, there she was again, ready to try something new. When that didn't work either, I'd leave class thinking that certainly this was the last we'd see of her. But the next day, there she was again, embodying openness and acceptance, and ready to try something else. She had an unrelenting vigor about her, a fierce and impervious tenacity that fueled her fire to keep showing up. She did not give up on us. Instead, she humbled herself, became a student of her students, and did the slow and difficult work of building bridges into our lives, giving us a glimpse of our possibilities, changing our beliefs about ourselves and the world, and helping us find our voice and our path and our place.

Because of the help of this one teacher, Erin Gruwell, many of my classmates are now successful in life. Her love for us, and her ceaseless determination to teach us against all odds, planted seeds in us that are still growing to this day. We are fathers, mothers, teachers, lawyers, doctors, pilots, entrepreneurs, real estate agents, coaches, and so much more. Furthermore, many of us are now paying it forward. A number of my friends from our original Freedom Writer class are now teachers and coaches themselves. In fact, one of my friends, Sharaud, is now a teacher, a track coach, and a law student. Not too long ago, his students, who live in one of the poorest neighborhoods in Long Beach, had the highest math scores in the district for three years in a row. As I've mentioned, I am now on the road, speaking or teaching 200 to 300 days per year all over the world. I have been blessed to work in most major cities in 48 states and on 4 continents. No matter where I go, whether I'm in Houston or Hong Kong, Kansas City or Cairo, Los Angeles or London, I am doing my best to carry a torch of inspiration into the recesses of dormant potential, and show the gems that are sparkling there. I am doing my absolute best to give others the hope that my teachers and other loving adults gave me.

Accept and Embrace Your Power

All that I share in this book is shared not to impress you with my success but to impress upon you just how much power you have to help your students turn the page and write new, more fulfilling chapters in their lives.

You have the power to help your students see that their lives can get better. You have the power to help them see that they are loved, that they matter, that they are here for a reason. You, my friend, have the power to make this world a better place through your work as a teacher. You have the power to change the world—one word, one act of kindness, one gesture of love, and one student at a time.

So please take possession of your power to make this world a better place—a place where no one is homeless or hungry or hopeless; a place where the least, the last, the lost, and the left out of our world are loved. Please, I beg you. Love, work, serve, and teach like *your* life depends on it, because your kids' lives actually do. Keep showing up, and keep giving your best. Hollywood probably won't make a movie about you, and you probably won't make a lot of money, but your living, with whatever remaining time you have on this earth, shall not be in vain.

Acknowledgments

Even on Your Worst Day, You Can Be a Student's Best Hope comes out of my life as a student, a teacher, and a speaker. It also comes from all of the people who, in one way or another, have helped me grow into the man I am today.

I would like to thank Dr. Robert Priest, my anthropology professor, who taught me about the power and importance of doing ethnographic fieldwork and cultural anthropology. I would also like to thank Dr. Craig Ott, a mentor and friend, who helped me think more critically about contextualizing communication. My education professor, Dr. James Pluedemann, inspired me to think more critically about how culture influences education and leadership. He introduced me to the tools required to analyze and evaluate the behavioristic presuppositions guiding many schools, and he helped me consider how developmentalism could be a healthier alternative in education. I would also like to thank Dr. Tite Tienou, one of the most inspiring men I know, who taught me to wrestle with theories about ethnicity and identity and their implications for our world today. I also need to express my gratitude for Dr. Duane Elmer for giving me a framework to think about communication in terms of culture.

I would like to express my most heartfelt thanks to the wonderful team at ASCD, who have helped bring this book to life. A few years ago, Genny Ostertag approached me at ASCD's fall Conference on Educational Leadership in Orlando about writing a book to help teachers, principals, administrators, and staff reach and teach more students. However, being in the middle of a 250-day speaking tour while juggling my role as a husband, father, homeschool teacher, and doctoral student, I did not have the time to commit to such an undertaking. Then, at ASCD's 2016 Annual Conference in Atlanta, Genny approached me again, along with Susan Hills, and they both encouraged me to write this book. Their belief in me truly honored me and convinced me to make the writing of this book a priority. Working with Susan on the first draft of the book was a delight, as she helped me to frame what I wanted to say and capture in writing some of my best, most meaningful ideas about helping youth. Finally, Katie Martin, the senior editor on this project, whose love of language enabled her to hear my heart, enhanced my voice and helped to make it sing and sting. For all of the ASCD team, I am so grateful.

I owe my greatest debt of thanks to my wife and children. The unconditional love of my three children—Manuel, Christopher, and Berkeley—and their willingness to share me with the world means so much to me. Hearing their heartbeats and seeing their little smiling faces after a long, hard, and exhausting speaking tour or book-writing session reminds me that the best things in life really are free.

And then there is my dear wife, Alice. When I had nothing but small pockets and big dreams, she was there, believing in me. When I stood on stages all over the world, trying to be a voice for the voiceless, she was there, standing with me.

When I wasn't making any money, and I didn't know how we were going to pay our bills, she found a job and supported us for two years and never, ever made me feel like less of a man because of it. When I've been helplessly sick, bed-bound and burdened, she's been there, never complaining, nursing me back to health. When, after giving my all to audiences, I've been empty and exhausted, unpleasant and unavailable, she's been there—every single time—praying for me, singing to me, keeping the kids quiet for me, loving me back to life. For her, words fail me. For her, thank you is not enough.

References

Androzzo, A. B. (1956). If I can help somebody. *Mahalia Jackson in concert (Easter Sunday 1967)*. Retrieved from songlyrics.com.

Devito, D., Shamberg, M., Sher, S. (Producers), & LaGravense, R. (Writer/Director). (2007). *Freedom writers* (Motion picture). United States: Paramount Pictures.

Geertz, C. (1977). *The interpretation of cultures*. New York: Basic Books.

Merriam, S. B. (2007). *Non-Western perspectives on learning and knowing: Perspectives from around the world*. Malabar, FL: Krieger.

Nisbett, R. (2003). *The geography of thought: How Asians and westerners think differently . . . and why*. New York: Free Press.

Vygotsky, L. S. (1978). *Mind in society: The development of higher psychological processes* (Revised ed.). (M. Cole, V. John-Steiner, S. Scribner, & E. Souberman, Eds.) Cambridge, MA: Harvard University Press.

Wintle, W. D. (1905). Thinking. Retrieved from https://allpoetry.com/poem/8624439-Thinking-by-Walter-D-Wintle

Index

About the Author

 **Manny Scott** is the founder of Ink International, Inc., an education consulting firm focused on empowering individuals to improve their lives and the lives of those around them, helping increase student achievement and leader effectiveness, and helping prevent dropouts and suicides. An original Freedom Writer, whose story is told in part in the movie *Freedom Writers*, Scott speaks at conferences, conventions, and schools worldwide. He is the author of *Your Next Chapter* and *How to R.E.A.C.H. Youth Today*, and he has energized more than a million leaders, educators, volunteers, and students worldwide with his authentic, inspiring messages of hope. You may reach him at MannyScott.com or at info@MannyScott.com.

Related ASCD Resources

At the time of publication, the following resources were available (ASCD stock numbers in parentheses):

PD Online® Courses
Embracing Diversity: Effective Teaching (2nd ed.) (#PD11OC123M)
Teaching with Poverty in Mind (#PD11OC139M)

Print Products
Better Than Carrots of Sticks: Restorative Practices for Positive Classroom Management by Dominique Smith, Douglas Fisher, and Nancy Frey (#116005)
Building Equity: Policies and Practices to Empower All Learners by Dominique Smith, Nancy Frey, Ian Pumpian, and Douglas Fisher (#117031)
Fostering Resilient Learners: Strategies for Creating a Trauma-Sensitive Classroom by Kristen Souers with Pete Hall (#116014)
Keeping It Real and Relevant: Building Authentic Relationships in Your Diverse Classroom by Ignacio Lopez (#117049)
Managing Your Classroom with Heart: A Guide to Nurturing Adolescent Learners by Katy Ridnouer (#107013)
Meeting Students Where They Live: Motivation in Urban Schools by Richard Curwin (#109100)
Teaching to Strengths: Supporting Students Living with Trauma, Violence, and Chronic Stress by Debbie Zacarian, Lourdes A. Alvarez-Ortiz, and Judie Haynes (#117035)

For up-to-date information about ASCD resources, go to www.ascd.org. You can search the complete archives of *Educational Leadership* at www.ascd.org/el.

ASCD myTeachSource®
Download resources from a professional learning platform with hundreds of research-based best practices and tools for your classroom at http://myteachsource.ascd.org/

For more information, send an e-mail to member@ascd.org; call 1-800-933-2723 or 703-578-9600; send a fax to 703-575-5400; or write to Information Services, ASCD, 1703 N. Beauregard St., Alexandria, VA 22311-1714 USA.

WHOLE CHILD
TENETS

The ASCD Whole Child approach is an effort to transition from a focus on narrowly defined academic achievement to one that promotes the long-term development and success of all children. Through this approach, ASCD supports educators, families, community members, and policymakers as they move from a vision about educating the whole child to sustainable, collaborative actions.

Even on Your Worst Day, You Can Be a Student's Best Hope relates to the healthy, safe, and engaged tenets. *For more about the ASCD Whole Child approach, visit* **www.ascd. org/wholechild.**

1 HEALTHY
Each student enters school healthy and learns about and practices a healthy lifestyle.

2 SAFE
Each student learns in an environment that is physically and emotionally safe for students and adults.

3 ENGAGED
Each student is actively engaged in learning and is connected to the school and broader community.

4 SUPPORTED
Each student has access to personalized learning and is supported by qualified, caring adults.

5 CHALLENGED
Each student is challenged academically and prepared for success in college or further study and for employment and participation in a global environment.